A

DISSERTATION

ON THE

LAW of NATURE, the LAW of NATIONS, and the CIVIL LAW in general.

Together with ſome

OBSERVATIONS

ON THE

Roman CIVIL LAW in particular:

To which is added, by Way of

APPENDIX,

A

Curious CATALOGUE of *Books*, very uſeful to the Students of theſe ſeveral Laws, together with the CANON LAW.

Fred B. Rothman & Co.
LITTLETON, COLORADO
1980

ISBN: 0-8377-0510-X

This book has been digitally archived to maintain the quality of the original work for future generations of legal researchers by William S. Hein & Co., Inc.

This volume printed on acid-free paper by William S. Hein & Co., Inc.

Printed in the United States of America.

A DISSERTATION ON THE LAW of NATURE, the LAW of NATIONS, and the CIVIL LAW in general.

Together with ſome

OBSERVATIONS ON THE *Roman* CIVIL LAW in particular:

To which is added, by Way of

APPENDIX,

A

Curious CATALOGUE of *Books*, very uſeful to the Students of theſe ſeveral Laws, together with the CANON LAW.

LONDON:

Printed for J. ROBERTS, *near the* Oxford Arms *in* Warwick Lane. M.DCC.XXIII.

Price *One Shilling* and *Six Pence*.

An Explanation of the Marginal Quotations from the Books of the Civil and Canon Law.

And First of the Civil Law.

THE *Institutes of* Justinian, *Book the First, Title the Second, Section, or Paragraph, the third and fourth.* I. 1. 2. 3, & 4.

Digest, Book the First, Title the Second, Law the Third, and Paragraph, or Section, the Fourth. D. 1. 2. 3. 4.

Digest, Book the First, Title the Second, Law the Third. Pr. *in* principio, *and* fin. *in* fine ejusdem legis. D. 1. 2. 3. *Pr. Fin.*

Digest, Book the First, Title the Second, and Laws the Third and Fourth. D. 1. 2. 3 & 4.

Meaning, Law the First, Section, or Paragraph, beginning with the Word Furtum, ff. *signifies the Digest, and the Words* de Furtis *denote the Title thereof.* L. 1. 33. *Furtum*, ff. *de Furtis.*

That is to say, Bartolus *on the first Law of the* Digests, *Book the Second, and Title the Fourth.* *Bart.* in l. 1. d. 2. 4.

Code, Book the First, Title the Twelfth, Law the Eighth, and Section, or Paragraph, the Second. C. 1. 12. 8. 2.

That is to say, Baldus *on the Fourth Law of the* Code, *Book the Sixth, and Title the Tenth.* *Bald.* in l. 4. C. 6. 10.

The Novels, Constitution the Eighty Ninth, and Chapter the Ninth. *Nov.* 89. c. 9.

Authentick, Collation the Ninth, Title the Ninth, and Novel Twenty. *Auth.* 9. 9. 20.

All these Books of the *Civil* Law are sometimes quoted by the initial Words of the Law it self; and by the Words of the Title: As, *Qui totam Hæreditatem*, for *De acquir. vel omit. Hæred.* That is to say, *The First Law of the Digest, Book 29, and Title the Second.*

Marginal Quotations from the Books of the *Canon* Law explain'd.

X.1.9.6.4. THAT *is to say, Book the First, Title the Ninth, Chapter the Sixth, and Paragraph the Fourth, of the Decretals of* Gregory.

VI. 3. 4. 23. *Book the Third, Title the Fourth, and Chapter the Twenty Third, of the Sixth Book of the Decretals, by Pope* Boniface *the Eighth.*

Cl. 2. 5. 2. *Book the Second, Title the Fifth, and Chapter the Second, of the* Clementines.

Extra 14. 3. *That is to say, Title the Fourteenth, and Chapter the Third, of the* Extravagants *of Pope* John *the Twenty Second.*

Com. 3. 2. *That is to say, Book the Third, and Chapter the Second of the* Communes.

Dist. 76. c. 2. *Distinction the Seventy Sixth, and Chapter the Second, of the first Part of the* Decrees: *and if a* V *Consonant, or this Note be added,* viz. §. *it denotes the Verse or Paragraph of that Chapter, as* Dist. 16. c. 2. v. 3. *or* §. 3.

16 Q. 7. 3. *That is to say, Cause the Sixteenth, Question the Seventh, and Chapter the Third, of the Second Part of the Decrees.*

Con. 1. 2. *Distinction the First, and Chapter the Second of the Third Part of the Decrees.*

All these Books of the *Canon* Law are likewise sometimes quoted by the initial Words of the Law, or Chapter it self; and by the Words of the Title: As thus, *Ex specialis*, extra *de Judæis.* That is to say, *Cap.* 17. *Tit.* 6. of the Fifth Book of *Gregories* Decretals. For the Word *Extra* imports these *Decretals* as well as the *Extravagants.*

A DISSERTATION ON THE Law of Nature, THE Law of Nations, &c.

IT having been a received Cuſtom and Uſage among the Doctors of the *Civil* Law, in the firſt Place, to diſcourſe of ſuch Things as are preparatory to other Matters, leading to the Knowledge of the Law, I have thought fit in the Beginning of the following Diſſertation to ſpeak of Laws in general, and of the Etymology and Derivation of the *Latin* Words *Lex* and *Jus*, that we may truly diſtinguiſh, what is meant thereby in a ſtrict and proper Acceptation of thoſe Terms. And having thus prepared a way for the enſuing Treatiſe, I ſhall in the next Place endeavour to ſpeak of the Law of Nature, the Law of Nations, and of the Civil Law in general, as it is common to this or that State and Country, together with some Observations on the *Roman* Civil Law in particular. Therefore, that I may proceed in due Order and Method, I shall divide this whole Treatise of Laws in general, into three Parts: Wherein, I shall, *First*, Treat of such Things, as belong to a *Preceptive* and a *Penal* Law; and to the Cessation or Repealing thereof. *Secondly*, I shall handle the Business of Dispensations, whereby a Man is discharg'd and exempted from the Obligation and Penalty of Laws. And, *Thirdly*, I shall say something in brief of Privileges; and of the Force and Effect of them in general. And,

First, A Law is in *Latin*, according to *Suarez*, *Tho. Aquinas*, *Valentia*, and others, stiled *Lex*, from the Verb *Ligo*, which signifies *to bind*; because Men are bound and obliged by Laws either to do, or not to do something. Wherefore a Law, in the Scripture Phrase, is called a Yoke, and a Bond. As for Example, *Let us break their Bonds in sunder, and cast away their Yokes or Cords from us* *. And again in the Prophecy of *Nahum*, *I will break his Yoke from off thee, and burst thy Bonds in sunder* †. But, *Isidore*, in his second Book of *Etymologies*, Chapter the Tenth, and some others do say; That the Word *Lex* is derived from the Verb *Lego*, signifying *to read*; because a Law is read and published in Writing, in order to be often read over for the Instruction and Illustration of the Mind, according to that of the *Psalmist* ||, *The Commandment, or Law of the Lord, is bright, enlightening the Eyes of those that behold it* *. Yet Writing is not essential to a Law, as I shall ob-

* Psalm 2. *ver.* 3.

† Chap. 1. *ver.* 13.

|| Psal. 19.

* *ver.* 8.

obſerve hereafter. For as a Cuſtom has the Force of a Law, and do's oblige as ſuch, tho' not reduc'd into Writing; ſo likewiſe a Law may have the Force and Power of a Law, and oblige as ſuch, though it be not expreſſed in Writing: Yet, for the Reaſon above-given, a Law is uſually drawn into Writing. *Cicero* in the firſt Book of his Treatiſe of Laws, will have it; That the Word *Lex* has its Original from the *Latin* Verb *Deligo*, to elect and chuſe; becauſe it teaches us, what we ought to elect and make choice of. But what we in *Engliſh* ſtile *Law*, is in the *Latin* denoted by ſeveral Names and Appellations: As ſometimes by the Word *Jus*, not only becauſe the Law deſigns and preſcribes that which is juſt, but alſo becauſe it gives unto every one that which is his Right, in *Latin* called *Jus*, according to the Determination of Juſtice: Which is a Vertue, that gives unto every Man that which is his Right to have and enjoy, as I ſhall ſhew by and by. Sometimes it is called a Conſtitution, Statute, or Sanction; tho' properly ſpeaking a Law and a Statute is not the ſame Thing: For a Law is properly ſaid to be that which is made by ſome Sovereign Prince or Supream Power, as by ſome Emperor, King, or by the whole State of the People: But a Statute is ſaid to be that which is made by an Inferior Prince, or by a State that is ſubject to a Prince, *&c.* As the Statutes of ſome Towns and Cities are: Thus we ſay, the Statutes of *Millain*, and the Statutes of *Mantua*, and the like.

But tho' the *Latin* Words *Jus* and *Lex* are often made uſe of in our Law Books, as Synonymous Terms, to ſignify the ſelf ſame Thing; yet there is ſome kind of Difference and Distinction, which we ought to make between them. For the *Latin* Word *Jus* is a generical Term, and has a Respect even unto those Laws, which are not reduc'd into Writing; and of this kind, we may reckon general and particular Customs, the Law of Nature, and the like: But the *Latin* Word *Lex* is restrain'd to a more special Signification and Meaning, having only a Regard to that Part of the Law, which is committed to Writing, for the Reason above-mention'd. I will here discourse of both in their just and proper Significations. And,

First, Of the Word *Jus*, which seems to be so called by the Figure *Apocope*, from the *Latin* Word *Jussu*; because it commands something to be done, or not to be done. For properly speaking, that is called *Jus*, which is the Command of Nature, or of the State, or of him that represents the State and Commonwealth. There are four other Acceptations deriv'd from this Sense and Meaning of the Word *Jus*, which are less proper; *Namely*, The Word *Jus* is sometimes by a *Metonymy* of the Thing contain'd, put for the Thing containing, made use of to denote the Art and Knowledge of the Law. *Secondly*, By the same Figure, (tho' by the way of Conversion) it is taken for that, which is of Right given unto every one thereby as his Due, and in this Sense it signifies a *Right*. *Thirdly*, It is taken in a particular Manner for that Power which the Law gives unto any Person; and in this Sense it signifies the same as *Power* or *Administration*: And this happens, as often as the Right and Power of doing any Thing is added to the Word *Jus*. *Fourthly*, It is taken for that Place, wherein the Law is administred,

vulgar-

vulgarly called a *Court of Judicature:* As when we say *in Jus vocare,* that is, to summon a Person into Court; and *in Jure Confessos pro judicatis haberi,* or in *English,* such Person, as do make a Confession in Court, are deem'd as Persons already adjudg'd and condemn'd. Wherein the Metonymy of the *Adjunct* is taken for the *Subject.* But, according to the proper Signification of the Word *Jus,* the same is defin'd and given to every Constitution, that commands Things right and decent to be done, and that forbids the contrary, by imposing a necessary Obedience on those for whom such Law was made and ordain'd. And herein we have two special Parts, *viz.* The Command it self, and the Execution of this Command. For it is the Business and Province of the Law, not to command every Thing, but only such Things as are honest, right and decent to be done, and to forbid the contrary. Now that is said to be Right, which is just and honest in it self, and of its own Nature: As, for Instance, to worship God; to hurt and injure no one: And also, that which conduces to the Profit and Advantage of the Community, as *Usucapion,* &c. The Execution of this Command consists in two Things, *viz.* in some Punishment added to the Law; and in the Authority of the Person that enacts a Law. In this Place, I understand the Word *Pœna* or Punishment in a very general Sense: So that an Action, which we commence against any one, is contain'd under that Name and Appellation. The Distribution and Dispensing of Law shew us, in whose Hands the Authority of enacting a Law consists, and where the Power is lodged.

Again, The Word *Jus* is taken in ſeveral other Senſes, not before mention'd. For *Firſt*, It ſignifies that which is always founded on Equity and good Conſcience, as the immutable Law of Nature is. *Secondly*, It denotes that which is for the Profit and Advantage of all Perſons in general; as the Law of Nations is. *Thirdly*, It imports that which is for the Profit of all Perſons, or (at leaſt) of the greateſt Part of the People, living in any particular State or Commonwealth; as the Civil Law is, according to the general Senſe thereof: And in this Senſe we underſtand the Common Law of *England*. So that the Word *Jus*, in this Diviſion, includes a Threefold Law, *viz.* The Law of *Nature*, the Law of *Nations*, and the *Civil* Law, according to the general Acceptation thereof. *Fourthly*, We uſe the Word *Jus* to denote the ſame, as *Neceſſitudo*, or a nearneſs of Relation: And thus we ſay in our Law-Books, *Jus Cognationis*, or *Affinitatis*. *Fifthly*, As the Edict of the *Roman* Prætors were ſtiled *Jus Honorarium*; ſo were the Sentences of every Judge ſtiled by the *Latin* Appellation of *Jus*. Yea, tho' the Judge ſhou'd pronounce an unjuſt Decree or Sentence; yet they were ſtill ſo called, without conſidering what the Judge has done, but what he ought to have done: And from hence proceeds this Term of Speech in our Law Courts, *viz. Jus dicere*, or (in *Engliſh*) to pronouce a Sentence. I have before obſerv'd, that the Place where the Judge or any other Magiſtrate ſits for the diſpatch of Juſtice, and for the ſake of pronouncing Judgment, is ſometimes in *Latin* called *Jus*: And this is true, tho' it be at the

Judges

Judges own Houſes, or upon a Journey, and the like.

But the Word *Lex* is not taken in ſo large and general a Signification, as the Word *Jus*: For it has either only the ſame Force and Meaning with the Word *Jus*, in reſpect of the two firſt Significations of this Word; or elſe it only imports the Form of a Contract, whether it be the Covenants or Conditions thereof. And hence proceeds this uſual way of Expreſſion in our Law-Books, *viz. Eâ Lege vel Conditione.*

But waving all other Acceptations of theſe two Terms, I ſhall come nearer to my preſent Purpoſe, and ſhew; that this Word *Jus*, in the general Senſe thereof, is taken in a threefold Manner, as above-remembred, *viz. Firſt*, For the Law of Nature, which is innate and born with Man. *Secondly*, For any poſitive Law whatſoever, whether it be of Divine or Humane Appointment. And, *Thirdly*, It is taken in the proper Senſe of the Word hereafter made uſe of, namely, for the *Roman* Civil Law. The Law of Nature, which I ſhall diſcourſe of by and by, is (as it were) the Foundation of the Law of Man; being that which Nature has taught all living Creatures, in the ſtricteſt Senſe thereof; that is to ſay, it is that Law, which is ſo expreſs'd in the Nature of all living Creatures, that it is not proper to Men alone, but by a kind of Similitude or Analogy, is common to Men with Brutes: As the Conjunction of Man and Woman, the Procreation and Education of Children, Self-Preſervation, *&c. Ariſtotle* in the fifth Book of his *Ethicks*, defines it to be that

Law, which retains its Force in all Places, and among all Nations; and is that which is ratify'd and confirm'd neither by Opinion, nor Learning; nor is it made null and void thereby. And *Cicero* in his first Book *De Legibus*, defines it to be the highest Pitch of human Reason; which, being planted in Man's Nature from the beginning, commands such Things as ought to be done, and forbids the contrary: But more of this immediately.

The Law, according to *Tho. Aquinas*, and some of the Doctors, may be divided into four Parts or Members, *viz.* into the Law Eternal, the Law of Nature, the positive Law of God, and the Law of Man. The Law Eternal, taken in a large Sense, is the Divine Will and Understanding it self, which ordain'd all Things from Eternity, according to *Solomon* in his Book of *Proverbs*; where speaking of Wisdom, he says *, *The Lord possessed me in the beginning of his way before his Works of old: I was set up from everlasting, and before the Earth was:* But taken strictly, it is the Mind and Reason of God, commanding Things that are Good, and forbidding Things that are Evil. Wherefore Sin is defin'd to be every Thing, which is said, done, or coveted, contrary to the Eternal Law or Will of God.

* Chap. 8. ver. 22, & 23.

The Law of Nature is the Agreement or Disagreement of a Thing it self with right Reason. And from hence it is, that the Disagreement which a Lie or Adultery has with right Reason, is the Law of Nature it self, which prohibits a Lie, and every Act of Adultery. Again, thus the Agreement, which the Preservation of our Neighbours Reputation has with

with right Reaſon it ſelf, may be ſtiled the Law of Nature, which commands and dictates the preſerving of our Neighbours Reputation. Some of the Doctors indeed define the Law of Nature to be the Light and Dictates of our Reaſon, whereby we know what Things ought to be done, and what ought not to be done. But this Definition (I think) do's not ſeem to be *à priori*, but *à poſteriori*. For the Law of Nature, *a priori*, ſeems to be the Agreement or Diſagreement of a Thing it ſelf, which we know by the Light of Nature. Now the Law of Nature in its extended Senſe is twofold, as I ſhall here obſerve. For the firſt is ſaid to be evident of it ſelf, and to ſtand in need of no Demonſtration; the firſt Principles of the Law of Nature being theſe, *viz.* That every Good ought to be embrac'd and purſued; and every Evil ought to be ſhunn'd and avoided, and the like. The ſecond Diviſion is that whoſe Principles are not ſo clear and ſelf-evident. For there may be ſome natural Laws aſſign'd, which are ſo obſcure and unknown to ſome Men, that they may be excus'd from the Tranſgreſſion thereof through an invincible Ignorance. But barring Ignorance, the Law of Nature is of ſo great Force and Efficacy, that it obliges all Perſons (in good Conſcience) having the uſe of human Reaſon, wheresoever they live, exiſt, and have their Being. Unleſs (perchance) they are excuſed in ſome particular Caſe, by Reaſon of ſome extraordinary ſupervening Circumſtances. The Law of Nature is immutable in Reſpect of its ſelf; and indeed always obliges under the Continuance of the ſame Circumſtances, the Matter thereof of not being changed in any wise: Because the Law of Nature consists in such Things themselves, as do either agree or disagree with right Reason. Therefore, if the Things themselves, and the Circumstances of Things be not changed, the same Agreement or Disagreement still remains: And, consequently, the Law of Nature cannot be changed, under the Continuance of the same Circumstances. Yet, I grant, that the Things themselves, and the Circumstances of Things may be so changed, that even the Law of Nature it self may be said to vary and be changed, as appears by Induction. For by the Dictates of the Law of Nature it is manifest, that it is not lawful to drink Wine, when Drunkenness may be surely foreseen to ensue thereupon: Yet if it be necessary to drink a strong and generous Wine on the score of Health, the drinking thereof is lawful, tho' Drunkenness be foreseen, and ensues thereon. For here a Circumstance supervenes, which renders the drinking of Wine lawful, tho' Drunkenness should ensue thereupon; for Drunkenness was not intended, but only permitted for a just Cause of Health. Again, though it be not lawful for one Man to purloin, and take away another's Goods against the Owner's Will; yet on the Circumstance of extream Necessity (according to some) this is lawful. *Thirdly*, God may permit some Things, which without his Permission are contrary to the Law of Nature: As a Bill of Divorce, and a Pleurality of Wives was heretofore lawful by the Divine Permission. For as God may vary and change the Things themselves, so he may likewise change the Law of Nature in

some

ſome Reſpect, where ſuch Change is not contrary to the Divine Attributes: And as he may ſupply that which the Law of Nature dictates and preſcribes; ſo he may alſo diſpenſe with this Law in ſome Degree. For whereas a Pleurality of Wives was contrary to the Law, which preſcribes and dictates the pacifick Government of a Family; yet, notwithſtanding this, God might ſupply the Law of Nature in this Part, by a pacifick Government of the Family immediately from himſelf: So that it follows from hence, That God may permit, and allow of a Pleurality of Wives. *Fourthly*, Homicide by a Man's own private Authority is unlawful; but yet if it be done in defence of a Man's own proper Life, *cum moderamine inculpatæ tutelæ*, it is lawful. And ſo it is, if it be done by God's Authority, who is the Lord of Life, and of all our Subſtance; as in the Caſe of *Abraham*, who by God's Command put his own Son to Death. *Laſtly*, It appears by the Law of Nature, That a *Depoſitum* ought to be reſtor'd to the Owner or Proprietor thereof upon Demand: But yet a Caſe may be aſſign'd, wherein ſuch a *Depoſitum* ought not to be thus reſtor'd, nay, the Law of Nature forbids us the Reſtitution of it; as when a Sword or other Weapon depoſited, is demanded to kill another Perſon. Some Perſons indeed have doubted, whether God can diſpenſe with this Law? But to them I anſwer, That he may diſpenſe with this Law in all thoſe Things, which ſo depend on him, and may be ſo chang'd, that all Things ſeem lawful by ſuch an Alteration: As when ſuch a Change and Alteration do's not appear repugnant to Reaſon, or contrary to his Attributes,

butes, as aforesaid. Thus God permitted a Pleurality of Wives unto the *Jews* or *Hebrews*, which tho' contrary to the Law of Nature in some Sense; yet it was not in the least repugnant to Reason, or his own Attributes. Therefore God may dispense with this Law in those Things, which so depend on and may be so changed, that they seem lawful by such a Change. But God cannot dispense with Blasphemy, Falshood, Idolatry, and the like, which are Sins of such a wicked Nature, that their Malice and Iniquity cannot be taken away by a Dispensation, tho' they may be pardon'd.

The Divine Law, is that positive Law which has Force, so far only, as it proceeds from God. And this is twofold, *viz.* The old Law, otherwise called the *Law of Moses*; and the new Law, commonly stiled the *Gospel Law.* Again, the Divine Law may be sub-divided into the Divine Law of Nature, of which I have already spoken; and the Divine Law positive. The Divine Law of Nature, is that which commands the same Thing as the Law of Nature does, and is contain'd in the Decalogue, and its Precepts. The divine positive Law, is that which commands something not ordain'd or enacted by the Law of Nature. Thus a previous Confession of our Sins is commanded before receiving the Eucharist, by him who has a Conscience pricked with Sin. And this Precept is called a divine positive Precept; because Confession of Sin, before receiving the Eucharist, is not enjoyn'd by the Law of Nature, but only by the express Law of God.

A Human Law is that which is made and eſtabliſh'd by Man's Authority, but yet notwithſtanding this has its Dependance upon God: For Men make Laws by that Power, which God has communicated to them, to the end that Subjects may be the better govern'd, and kept within their Duty; and, through a Fear of Puniſhment, be reſtrain'd from the Commiſſion of Sin. Now a human Law is twofold, *viz. Secular* and *Eccleſiaſtical.* A *Secular* Law is that which is enacted by the Power of ſecular Perſons; as Emperors, Kings, and the like. And an *Eccleſiaſtical* Law or Conſtitution, is that which is made by the Power of the Church, according to the *Canon* Law; as by the Pope, a General Council, and ſo forth. An *Eccleſiaſtical* Conſtitution is twofold, *viz. General* and *Special.* A *General* Conſtitution is the Sanction or Law of him, who has the Power and Right of making Decrees and Statutes for the Advantage of his Subjects, whether they be Laymen or Clerks, it matters not: And by thoſe all Perſons that are ſubject to the Enacting Power, are bound to the Obſervance of ſuch Law or Conſtitution *. A *Special* Conſtitution is by a proper Name called a *Privilege*, becauſe it is made in Favour of a private Perſon, or ſome private Affair; or elſe, becauſe it begets as it were a private Law unto ſuch particular Perſons, unto whom it is granted: And it is nothing elſe but a Command or Order, whereby ſome particular Matter is indulged in a particular Manner to the Perſons requeſted, and obtaining the ſame. The Decrees of General Councils are thoſe Acts, which are confirm'd by the Authority of the

* Diſt. 2. *Cap.* 3.

the Pope; as the Decrees of Provincial Councils are in Popish Countries confirm'd by the Authority of Patriarchs, Primates, and Metropolitanes of the same Province: And the Decrees, of which the whole *Canon* Law is said to consist, are called *Ecclesiastical* Constitutions; and are sometimes comprehended under the Name and Stile of *Canons* *. Thus there is one Kind of human Constitution, which is called *Civil*; and another, which is stiled *Ecclesiastical.* A *Civil* Constitution is in other Terms called a Civil Law, or in *Latin*, *Jus Forense* †; and is either *Common* or *Municipal.* That is called the *Common Civil Law*, which obliges all Persons, that were subject to the *Roman* Empire; and which we have contain'd in the Books of the *Civil* Law; and which cannot be made, unless it be by the Emperor, in Virtue of that Power, which was heretofore transferr'd on his Royal Majesty. A *Municipal* Law is that which every City, State, or Commonwealth, enacts for its own Use, on the Account of Things Divine and Human.

* Dist. 2. *Cap.* 2, & 3.

† Dist. 3. *Cap.* 1.

There is one Kind of Law stiled *Preceptive*; and another stiled *Penal.* A *Preceptive* Law is that which commands and enacts something to be done, or not to be done, without ordaining any Punishment. And a *Penal* Law is that which enacts something to be done, or not to be done, by ordaining a determinate Punishment to be inflicted on the Transgressors of that Law; or else, it leaves the Punishment to be determin'd by the Discretion of the Judge, according to the Quality of the Crime. Now a Punishment is ordained, to the End that Subjects, who are not induced through

Love

Love to the Obſervance of Laws, ſhould be induc'd thereunto, through Fear of Puniſhment. But whether a Judge can leſſen and diminiſh Puniſhments preſcrib'd by Law, or whether he is bound to impoſe the very ſame, I ſhall conſider in another Place, where I ſhall ſhow, that even an inferior Judge may leſſen and diminiſh Puniſhments, on the Account of ſome ſupervening Circumſtances, unleſs the Law expreſly forbids the Change and Alteration of the Puniſhment. *Alphonſus à Caſtro* reckons up ſeveral Reaſons, on which Account Puniſhments may be ſometimes increaſed, and ſometimes diminiſh'd by the Judge. Having conſider'd theſe Things, I ſhall next conſider whether a Penal Law obliges in Conſcience. Now, not only a *Preceptive*, but even a *Penal* Law, whereby ſomething (*viz.*) is commanded by Puniſhment, added to the Tranſgreſſion thereof, does oblige, unleſs it otherwiſe appears, that the Legiſlator did not deſign to oblige Men in Conſcience: But in this Concluſion, all the Doctors do not agree, but are divided into two Opinions. The firſt is that of *Jaſon*, *Decius*, *Gomez*, and others quoted by *Leſſius*, who think that a Civil Law does not oblige in Conſcience, when only a temporal, or corporal Puniſhment is therein decreed againſt the Tranſgreſſors thereof, although ſuch Puniſhment be ſevere and grievous, as the Loſs of an Eſtate, Life, and the like, provided it does not otherwiſe appear, that the Law-giver intended ſuch Law ſhould oblige in Conſcience, and that there be no Scandal or Contempt ſhewn thereunto. *Firſt*, Becauſe a Penal Law is an odious Law, and therefore ought to be ex-

explain'd with great Benignity, and as favourably as possibly may be, according to this Maxim or Rule of Law, viz. *Odia restringi, Favores convenit ampliari.* *Secondly,* Because the Legislator, by applying a temporal Punishment, is deem'd to exclude an eternal; for he that expresses one Thing, and is silent as to another, is deemed to exclude that Thing, unto which he is silent *. *Thirdly,* Because Subjects may probably think the Law-giver sufficiently contented with the Punishment he has express'd, and will not impose a greater Obligation on them, unless the same may be strongly inferred from his Intention. Therefore, though a Legislator may oblige *ad Pœnam & ad Culpam*, that is to say, under a Penalty, and in Conscience, yet whilst he only expresses a Penalty, and it do's not otherwise appear, that he design'd to oblige in Conscience, he is deem'd to oblige his Subjects only *ad Pœnam*; thinking the Commination of a temporal Punishment to be sufficient to hinder them from offending, and to keep them within their Duty, without a greater Restraint.

* X. 2.23. 5.

The Second Opinion is, that of *Suarez, Toletus, Salas*, and others; asserting, That a Penal Law do's oblige in Conscience, according to the Weight and Importance of the Matter thereof, unless it appears by some Means or other, that this was contrary to the Mind of the Legislator. *First*, Because a Law containing a Precept do's, according to some Casuists, oblige in Conscience; therefore since a Penal contains a Precept, it do's most certainly according to these Men oblige in Conscience. *Secondly*, Because a Punishment seems to suppose a Fault as often as any Thing is prohibited under a Penalty by him that has the Power of forbidding the ſame. *Thirdly*, Becauſe a Law or Precept do's hereby differ from Advice and Counſel, which do's not oblige in Conſcience as a Law or Precept do's. *Fourthly*, Becauſe the Holy Scripture, and the Fathers of the Church, do every where condemn the Violation of human Laws, tho' many of theſe Laws are no more than Penal*. Therefore, it is an Argument, that human Laws do oblige in Conſcience, becauſe when Legiſlators do not intend to oblige in any Thing, but what is commanded under Conſcience, they are wont to expreſs the ſame; therefore when they do not expreſs the ſame, ſaying they deſign not to oblige under Conſcience, they are deem'd to oblige under Conſcience. From hence it follows, that a Law for the Payment of Cuſtoms, under Pain of loſing and forfeiting the Goods imported, do's oblige in Conſcience: And ſo of other Laws, wherein a Puniſhment is added to be inflicted on the Tranſgreſſors. But more of this in another Place.

* 11 Q. 3. 98.

The Emperor *Juſtinian* deſigning to give an Account of the *Roman* Law in his *Inſtitutions*, which he cauſed to be compiled by Way of an Abridgment, thought fit to begin the ſame with a Treatiſe of *Juſtice* it ſelf, as being the *Baſis* and Foundation of all Law; dividing this Title of the Law into five Parts. In the firſt Part of this Title, he delivers a Definition of *Juſtice*. In the Second, he gives us a Definition of *Juris-Prudence*, or the Knowledge of the Law. In the Third, he declares by what Order and Method, Laws ought to be learn'd and treated of. In the Fourth, he describes the Precepts of the Law. And in the fifth Part of this Title, he gives us a Division of the *Law* it self. Therefore, having in the foregoing Sections or Paragraphs, explain'd the several Acceptations of the Words *Jus* and *Lex*, and given the Etymology of the latter Term, by way of Premises to this Discourse; I shall in the ensuing Dissertation, consider the five Divisions of this Title; and speak to each of them in the following Order, beginning with the Law. *Secondly*, I shall speak of *Justice*. *Thirdly*, Of the Divifion of the Law. *Fourthly*, Of *Juris-Prudence*, or the Knowledge of the Law. And, *Fifthly*, Of the Maxims and Method of explaining Laws: And this shall be the first Part of my general Design in treating of Laws.

Therefore to begin with the first Head of this Division, *viz*. The Law of Man, which is said to be the same Thing with a Civil, Positive and Written Law; I shall define it to be, that common Precept or Ordinance of Men, that have a Legislative Power vested in them of making Laws; whereby they provide for the civil Affairs of human Life, and punish Offences either wilfully or ignorantly committed: And this, in other Terms, is called *communis Reipub. sponsio.* Now this Law differs from the Law of Nature, because the Law of Nature is a general Law, but the Law of Man is understood to be a particular *Law*. The Law of *Nature* has its Demonstrations, and invincible Reasonings, but the *Law* of *Man* has only the arbitrary Will and Purpose of its Maker to support it. Again, The Law of *Nature* is every where the

the ſame, but the *Law* of *Man* ſtiled a poſitive Law, is not the ſame in all Places: To which the Reader may add, that the Law of *Nature* is Eternal, but *poſitive Laws* are mutable, and may be changed.

The Architechtonical Cauſe of the Law is *Juſtice*, which leads me to the ſecond Head of my Diviſion. Now *Juſtice* is defin'd to be a conſtant and perpetual Will or Purpoſe of giving unto every one his own Right. I ſhall not here treat of *Divine* Juſtice, but only of an external Kind of Juſtice commonly called *Civil* or *Political* Juſtice: Which only tends to the Forming of the Political Manners of Mankind in this Life, by requiring an external kind of Honeſty, that the Common-wealth may enjoy a ſafe Peace and Tranquility among Men. This kind of Juſtice (the Philoſophers ſay) is twofold. The Firſt is ſtiled *univerſal* Juſtice, it being that which comprehends all other Virtues. And the Second is called *Particular* Juſtice, as it is only one of the Moral Virtues. *Univerſal* Juſtice is wont to admit of a threefold Definition, according to the threefold Order and Reſpect of Man, as deſcribed in St. *Paul's Epiſtle* to *Titus*: Where he ſays, *For the Grace of God, which bringeth Salvation, hath appear'd unto all Men, teaching us; That denying Ungodlineſs and worldly Luſts, we ſhould live* Soberly, Righteouſly, *and* Godly *in this preſent World* *. That is to ſay, *Soberly* in Reſpect of our ſelves, and in a private Condition of Life; *Righteouſly* in Reſpect of other Men, and in a publick Station; and *Godly* in Reſpect of God and Religion. Therefore, the Firſt Order of *Univerſal* Juſtice, as it reſpects Man, is his Duty towards God;

* Chap 2. *ver.* 11 & 12.

unto whom he ought to yield Worship and Obedience, as being his Lord and Creator.

But I shall not here treat of *Universal*, but only of *Particular* Justice, which is opposite and contrary to injurious Dealing; and is divided into *Distributive* and *Commutative* Justice. The First of these relates to the Distribution of Rewards and Punishments, according to the Proportion and Variety of Men's *Merits* or *Demerits*. And the latter is employ'd about Contracts, and the equal Permutation of Things; and the two Parts of this Division make up what the Emperor stiles *Particular* Justice. Now Justice is rightly said to *be a perpetual Will*, &c. For tho' Matters and Cases do vary and change in so great a Diversity of Things; yet the Mind has certain Principles and *Ideas* naturally implanted in the Breasts of all Men, whereby it judges even according to a Diversity of Circumstances, *what is just*, &c. And these *Ideas* or Principles are perpetual and immutable: And when the Will is conformably obedient to these Principles, it may then be said to act in a just and regular Manner. As to that Part of the Definition, wherein it is said, that Justice *gives to every one that which is his due*: I say, this may be called the Property of Justice. And as *Particular* Justice is twofold, so likewise is the Essence of Justice twofold, *viz.* consisting in a Distribution of Rewards and Punishments for Merits done, and Crimes committed. And, *Secondly*, In the Equality of Commutation, that an Injury be done to no Person.

But the Word *Justice* in a Dissertation upon Law and Policy may be taken, even in a *legal* Sense and Acceptation, as well as in a *Divine* and

and *Moral* One; and then it is taken for *Juſtice* of *Works*, or (which is the ſame Thing) for *Obedience* due unto a Superior, or any other Magiſtrate; or elſe for that Order, whereby Men are ſubject and obedient unto Superiors: For Words ought to be underſtood according to the ſubject Matter of them. Therefore, touching the Etymology of the Word *Alciatus*, in the Firſt Book of his *Parergon Juris* *, thinks * Cap. 19 that *Juſtice* is ſo called, *quia vim ſiſtat*, that is to ſay, becauſe it hinders and puts a ſtop to Force and Violence. But *Hotoman*, in his Commentaries on the *Juſtinian* Inſtitutes †, will † I. 1. 1. have it ſo called, becauſe *in eâ Jus ſiſtatur*, that is to ſay, becauſe the Law has its Subſiſtence therein. And *Iſidore*, in his Treatiſe touching the Signification of Words ||, aſſures us; that || Cap. *Ferus. D. v.* 1. *Juſtice* is thus ſtiled, becauſe it is *quaſi Juris ſtatus*, the Law being founded thereon, and placed therein. Yet ſome maintain, 'tis more proper and ſimple to ſay *Juſtum à Jure*; and thus the Word *Juſtitia* is derived from the *genitive* Caſe of *Juſtum*, by adding the *Latin* Termination or Particle *(tia)* thereunto: As from *Mœſtum, Mœſti, Mœſtitia*; and from *Lœtum, Lœti, Lœtitia*. And therefore, in the Preface to the 69th Novel, we find the Word *Juſtitia* has its Name, and is ſo called from the Thing it ſelf, *viz.* from that Right which it gives to every one, as it is his Right. *Juſtice* is the Vertue it ſelf; and that which the Lawyers ſtile *Jus*, is the Exerciſe and Practice of that Vertue. *Juſtice* is ſaid to be the *Bonum ſupremum*, the Law is ſaid to be the *Bonum medium*, and *Juris-Prudence* is ſaid to be the *Bonum infimum* * * 12 Q. 2. S. *Juſtice* requires us to give every Man his due.

 the

the Law is co-assisting hereunto; and *Juris-Prudence* teaches us, how this may be done.

As Justice is taken in a twofold Sense, so likewise is Injustice understood in a twofold Manner: For *contrariorum eadem est Ratio & Disciplina.* There is one kind of Injustice; which being in Greek called Ἀνομία, is in *English* translated *universal Injustice*; and is what St. *John* in his first Epistle stiles a Transgression of the Law; and is sometimes in Holy Scripture called Ἀδικία, or *Unrighteousness* *. Now this kind of Injustice is an universal Disobedience, Contumacy and Contempt of all Things, or Laws founded upon Equity: Such as was that in the *Cyclops*, denying, that the Laws were made for them. *Particular* Injustice is taken in a more restrain'd Sense, for the defrauding of our Neighbour; which may happen even in those Men, that are otherwise accounted just in their Dealing: As *Cato* was accounted unjust in Plundering the Isle of *Cyprus*, and in laying violent Hands on himself; and *Brutus* in exposing *Thessalonica* and *Sparta* to the Ravage of the Soldiers. So on the contrary, by a Parity of Reason, *Universal* Justice is an Obedience paid unto all Laws both *Divine* and *Human, Civil* and *Natural*; and is that which is opposed unto that which we call Ἀνομία †, in which Sense Philosophers stile *Aristides* a just Man. *Secondly, Particular* Justice is that which defends and preserves the Order and Properties of particular Men; and renders an Equality in Contracts. And thus we say, that a Merchant or Tradesman, who do's not defraud his Chapman in the Dealings he has with him, is a just Man. As we also stile him a Man of Justice; who is fitly qualified

* Rom. ch. 1. *v.* 18.

† John 1. & 3. Rom. 1. & 2.

lified to be promoted to the Government, and Administration of publick Affairs. And in this Sense we find it taken in the Book of *Genesis* *, where *Jacob* says, *So shall my Righteousness answer for me, in the Time to come, or to morrow,* as the *Hebrew* Text has it.

* Chap. 30. v. 33.

Having thus distinguish'd the several Appellations of *Justice* into their proper Classes, I shall here briefly speak of them asunder. For *Universal* Justice may be reduced to three *Classes* or Orders. The first of these points out Man's Duty unto God; and is a Question, as it examines whether a Man can fulfil the Precepts of Universal Justice with a concomitant Grace, properly belonging to Theology. The second is that which regards the Order of Man in respect of himself; and this belongs to *Moral* Philosophy, though some will not have this to be the end of *Ethicks*; that being the common Part of *Ethicks*, from whence the Rules of *Oeconomicks* and *Politicks* are borrow'd. But this second Order do's not rightly seem to be consider'd under the Head of universal Justice, unless it be in an improper Manner. Therefore, the third Consideration is the only Business of a Lawyer. 'Tis here to be observ'd, that the Schoolmen have another Description of legal and universal Justice, defining it to be that Vertue, which perfects and qualifies a Man for the Service of his Country: But which way soever you take it, whether in this Sense, or that of *Aristotle*, *viz.* for a Complication of all Vertues, the Consideration of both of them belongs to the Knowledge of the Law, as consider'd in its own Nature. For the Knowledge and Explication of all Laws both publick and private do's hereunto belong, tho' we do not meet with it in the Body of the Civil Law.

The Law is defin'd to be *Ars boni & æqui*: where by the Word *Ars*, I mean such a Knowledge as is learn'd and acquir'd by Practice, and is profitable to human Life; it being partly collected from the Demonstration of practical Principles, and partly from the probable Arguments of sound Reasoning. The Words *Bonum* and *Æquum* are here taken, for an exact and perfect Equity founded upon good Conscience; or else for a certain general Rule of Justice: And as the Word *Bonum* relates to *universal* Justice; so the Word *Æquum* has a Respect to *particular* Justice. For the Word *Æquum* may be understood to denote that which is such by Nature; Equity being that part of Justice, which is taught us by the Law of Nature. But by the Word *Bonum* we understand that which is good and profitable unto Men, as they are Members of Civil Society, though it may sometimes seem to deviate a little from natural Equity.

Having thus far treated of *Justice*, and of the Terms *Lex* and *Jus*, I shall next in order proceed to discourse of what we call *Juris-Prudence*, or the Knowledge and Study of the Law. Now *Juris-Prudence* is defin'd to be the Knowledge of Things *Divine* and *Human*; and a good Discernment between that which is just, and that which is unjust. I call it the Knowledge, or *Notitia* of Things *Divine* and *Human*, because it do's for the most part consist in the Evidence and Demonstration of natural Principles and *Ideas*: And in *Latin* I call it *Scientia*, in the extended

Sense

Senſe of the Word, as it is an Art and Method; becauſe the Knowledge of Juſtice and Injuſtice is not acquir'd by common Senſe alone, or by the natural Ratiocination of the Mind; but 'tis even comprehended under a certain kind of Doctrine or Method of Learning, and under the Precepts of Civil Prudence.

All Laws are either of *Divine* or *Human* Authority, as I ſhall obſerve more at large hereafter. Among ſuch as are of Divine Authority, are the Law of Nature, and the Law of Nations, the Law of *Moſes*, the Law of the Prophets, and (among the *Papiſts*) the *Decretal* Epiſtles. But the Divine Law properly ſpeaking is that which is written in the Law of *Moſes*, and conſiſts of three Kinds of Precepts. Some of which are ſtiled *Moral*, and theſe as natural Precepts have a perpetual Duration and Continuance; notwithſtanding the Law of Grace. Some of them are *Judicial* and *Ceremonial*; and theſe have not been obſerv'd ſince the Law of Grace, or the Goſpel came into the World, unleſs it be ſuch alone as were renewed thereby. But *Ægid. Bellamer* remarks, that theſe Moral Precepts were precedent unto any written Law, tho' no Puniſhment was expreſly annex'd and inflicted for the Tranſgreſſion thereof: Temporal Puniſhment being only introduc'd ſince the Law was reduc'd into Writing. But ſome of the Judicial Precepts are ſtill obſerv'd among ſome Men in the World, notwithſtanding the *Law* of *Grace* or the *Goſpel.* As for Inſtance, that the Wife of a Brother deceas'd, cannot contract Matrimony with her firſt Husband's Brother. And alſo, that Tithes are due without any certain

Quan-

Quantity assign'd. The Law of God is also called the Law of natural Reason, as well as the Law and Precepts of *Moses*: And this was the *first* Law that was given to Mankind. The *second* Law was the Law of the Prophets, which is more properly treated of by *Divines* and *Theologists*; and therefore I shall leave it to them. The *third* Law was the Law of Kings and Emperors chosen by the People, containing many *Species*, as I shall shew by and by. Now these Laws of *Moses*, and the Prophets, were invented and reduc'd into Writing (as some will have it) in the second Age of the World. Again, we have another Law called the Divine Law of Grace, and this is the Gospel-Law abovementioned: I shall come hereafter to shew, wherein this Law of the Gospel corrects the Law of *Moses*; and in what Respect the Apostolical Law declares and explains the Law of the Gospel.

Again, there is one Law of Nature, called the *Law of Nature*, as it is common to all living Creatures. A *second*, which is called the *Law of Nature, according to that natural Reason which accrues unto all Mankind.* And a third, which is called the *Law of Nature as it were received.* And according to this Law, Wars were first made, and Dominions acquir'd, and the World was divided into divers Kingdoms, Principalities and States: And this is properly called the Law of Nations. And these three Kinds of Laws were in the World, long before any positive written Law was made.

The first Law that was invented and discover'd in the *Æra* of Time, when God created Man after his own Image, was called the Law of Nature, as aforesaid: And this is twofold,

viz.

viz. The Law of Nature, as it is common to all Things created; and the Law of Nature, as it respects a rational Being: Which is the same Distinction with that which the Doctors call the *Primary* and *Secondary* Law of Nature. For this *Primary* Law of Nature is the same with that which they sometimes stile the *Common* Law of *Nature*: And the *Secondary* Law of Nature is the same with that which they sometimes term the *natural Law* of *Reason*. Now this first *common* Law of Nature was deliver'd and made known unto Man at the very Time of his Creation, and the Creation of all other living Creatures made for the Service of Man, according to that Saying of the *Psalmist**; for which see the Psalm it self: And it is, therefore, stiled *Common*; because it is implanted both in Brutal, as well as Rational living Creatures without any Distinction. For this *Primary* or *Common* Law of Nature, in *Latin* called *Jus primævum naturale*, comprehends in it self a natural Kind of Instinct or Institution; As the Conjunction of Male and Female, the Procreation of an Off-spring, or the getting of Children, and the Education and Nurture of them; and all such other natural Appetites as are common to all Animals. And, *Secondly*, At the Time of Man's Creation, there was also another Law of Nature given us, which is called, the *Law* of *right Reason*, or the *Secondary* Law of Nature: And this is, therefore, called the *Law* of *right Reason*; because it is not common to Brutes, but only to such Persons as are endued with human or right Reason: And this is exemplify'd in our Religion towards God, in our Obedience towards our Parents, in Self-

Preser-

* Psalm 8. *v.* 6, &c.

Preſervation, and in a Love and Zeal for our Country, and the like. And upon this Law of Nature likewiſe depends that excellent natural Precept, of doing the ſame to another, that you would have done to your ſelf. Which was afterwards confirm'd to us both by the *old* Law, as well as by that of the *Goſpel* *, and (as St. *Paul* ſays) by the Law of the Apoſtles alſo †. Now this natural Law of *right Reaſon* is frequently called the *Law* of *Nations*, and ſometimes the *primary Law* of *Nations*; becauſe Nations, or Men alone, do only make uſe of this Law.

* Mat. ch. 7. Luke ch. 6.

† Gal. ch. 5.

At the Time when this *natural Law* of *right Reaſon* was firſt introduc'd in the World, there were no other Laws or Conſtitutions among Men to govern themſelves by; but Mankind liv'd in a State of Nature, and had all Things in Common among them: For *Bartolus*, and the Doctors, do all agree, that *Meum* and *Tuum* were then found out, and diſcover'd in the World, which have given Mankind ſo much Trouble ever ſince their firſt Diſcovery. And, according to this *Law* of *Nature*, Men liv'd for ſome Time, till they began to multiply and increaſe upon Earth, and to become injurious unto each others natural Right and Subſiſtence. For no ſooner did the Number of Mankind begin to increaſe and multiply (as aforeſaid) but the Malice and Wickedneſs of Men did likewiſe increaſe with them, inſomuch that they cou'd not live by this Law of Nature alone: Whereupon the Nations, and People of the Earth, did agree among themſelves upon certain Laws and Human Inſtitutions. And hence began the Diſtinction of Dominion and Proper-

ty

ty among Men, making certain Laws and Conſtitutions; that no one ſhou'd by way of Invaſion enter into another Man's Poſſeſſion: And from this Diſtinction of Property aroſe Wars, Captivity, and Services among Men. Hence alſo Nations began to contract with each other about Things thus divided and diſtinguiſh'd into Property: And by this means a third Law came into the World; which introduc'd Wars, Captivity, Services and Contracts. And this was properly ſtiled in *Latin* the *Jus Gentium*, and in *Engliſh*, the *Law* of *Nations*. Men liv'd on theſe three Kinds of Laws from the Time of *Adam*'s Creation till the Days of *Moſes*, excluſively: And this I call the firſt *Æra*, or the *Æra* before the Law of *Moſes*, within which Period of Time we had three Laws given us (as aforeſaid) *viz.* The *primary common* Law of *Nature*; The *ſecondary* Law of Nature, or the Law of *natural Reaſon*: And, *Laſtly*, The *Law* of *Nations*, in other Terms, called the *ſecondary* Law of Nature, becauſe the *primary* Law of Nations is the ſame with the Law of Nature aforeſaid. But of theſe more in another Place.

After this Period of Laws came the ſecond *Æra*, which is commonly called, *The Time under the Law*, wherein there were Three other *Species* of Laws deliver'd, *namely*, The *Law* of *Moſes*; the *Law* of the *Prophets*; and, the Civil Law in the general Senſe of the Phraſe. For when God ſaw the Malice of Men to abound on Earth, He himſelf gave a Law unto the World; and caus'd the ſame to be expreſs'd in Writing by his Servant *Moſes*, giving the Law unto *Moſes* upon Mount *Sinai*. And this is called the *Moſaick* Law, conſiſting of the ten Commandments;

ments: Or in other Terms, it is stiled the *Decalogue* Law; importing the same Thing as the Law of the ten Commandments. In this Law of *Moses* there are also some other Precepts which are called *Mystical*; that is to say, such Precepts as are deliver'd under Types and Figures: Some of which were *Sacramental*; and others only *Ceremonial*. Now these Precepts of the *Decalogue* are all immutable and eternal (saving one) and are called *moral* Precepts, because they respect the Manners of Men, and the Methods of living an honest and happy Life. Then in Process of Time there was added to this Law of *Moses* a second Law, called, The *Law* of the *Prophets*; which is the Law that (after the Pentateuch) runs throughout the remaining Part of the *Old Testament*. And tho' the Law of *Moses* and the *Prophets* be observed even to this Day, in respect of its *moral* Precepts; yet as to the *mystical* Precepts thereof, we find them both chang'd in some Respects, not only by the Gospel-Law, but even by the *Canon* Law too. *Calderinus* thinks, That the Law of *Moses* may be quoted in Courts of Judicature at this Time for the Decision of Causes; and ought to be observ'd in some particular Cases.

Afterwards, when the World grew more numerous, and daily increas'd in Wickedness (as aforesaid) it was found, that Men could not live by the Law of *Moses* and the *Prophets* alone: And therefore a new Law superven'd, which was called the *Civil Law*, in the general Notion of the Words. And this Law had its first Original from Kings, and other Rulers of the World, Men living by the Law of Nations (as already

already related) till this laſt Law came into the World. For it muſt be obſerv'd, that even by the *Law* of *Nations*, the People of the Earth choſe unto themſelves Kings, and other Governors of their reſpective States, according to their Humours, that they might be the more commodiouſly ruled, and protected by them, according to ſome Law: And to him they yielded Obedience; and were govern'd by the Laws, which their Kings and Princes made for them, which in the largeſt Senſe of the Words were ſtiled the Civil Law. And thus, according to *Baldus*, in his Treatiſe of Schiſm, Kings were originally by the Law of *Nations*; tho' the Nature, Extent, and Object of their Power, ariſes from the Civil and Municipal Laws of their reſpective Dominions; and is directed by it. And herewith agrees *Andreas Iſerne*, ſaying, That Kings were the firſt Lords and Rulers of the World, invented among Men by the *Law* of *Nations*, and continued by Civil and Municipal Laws. For though Emperors have been of a new Invention only, *viz.* ſince the Time of *Chriſt's* Incarnation, or then about: Yet Kings were ever, and at all Times, even long before our *Saviour's* Coming upon Earth. The firſt Emperor that ever was in the World, was *Octavianus*, commonly called *Auguſtus Cæſar*; who, according to Hiſtorians, reign'd Emperor at the Time of Chriſt's Coming in the Fleſh; tho' the Gloſs on the *Roman* Civil Law maintains, That *Julius Cæſar* was the firſt, and *Auguſtus* only the ſecond Emperor; as I ſhall ſhew hereafter, in treating of the *Roman* Law.

Theſe Kings being therefore thus created and elected, by the Conſent of the People, they made ſome fome Laws for the Government of the State, and for the Good of the Commonwealth, over which they prefided: And from hence the Civil Law, in the general Import thereof, had its firft Rife and Beginning; as aforefaid. Now, the firft King that gave Civil Laws to the *Grecians*, was King *Foraneus*: And hence, according to the Opinion of fome Men, we derive the *Latin* Word *Forus*; which fignifies a Place, or Court of Judicature. In the fame Manner King *Mercurius Trifmegiftus* gave Laws to the *Egyptians*, *Solon* to the *Athenians*, and *Lycurgus* to the *Lacedemonians*; and *Numa Pompilius* alfo gave fome Laws to the *Roman* People. And all thefe Laws were, therefore, called Civil Laws; becaufe each of the faid Commonwealths, in *Latin* ftiled *Civitates*, did make ufe of fome Law or other eftablifh'd by the Authority of the faid Kings. And thus *Rome* was govern'd by thefe kingly Laws till the Time of *Tarquinius Superbus*, the 7th King of *Rome*, who being depos'd for his Tyranny, the kingly Power was extinguifh'd in him, as I fhall elfewhere obferve, in difcourfing of the *Roman* Law. So that from what has been faid, it appears, That the *Civil Law*, in the large and general Acceptation of the Words, is that Law which has its Rife and Authority from the Civil Power; and the Civil Power is that which governs a Kingdom, State or Commonwealth. Thus if we confider the three *Æra*'s, or Periods of the Law, in refpect to its Invention, we fhall find, that there have been nine Tables or *Species* thereof, fince the Beginning of the World *, *viz*. The *Primary* and *Secondary* Law of *Nature*, and the Law of *Nations*, in the firft *Æra*. The

* Abb. in c. 1. x. 1. 1.

Law

Law of *Moses*, the Law of the Prophets; and the Civil Law, generally ſo called, in the ſecond *Æra*. And the Law of *Grace*, the *Civil* Law, ſtrictly ſo term'd, and the *Canon* Law, in the third *Æra*. I ſhall, in the enſuing Chapter, ſpeak of the *primary* and *ſecondary* Law of *Nature*, the Law of Nations, and the Civil Law, generally ſo called, *&c.*

CHAPTER *the Second.*

I HAVE obſerv'd in the foregoing Chapter, That the Law of Nature is twofold, *viz.* That which is commonly ſtiled the *primary* Law of *Nature*; and that which is ſtiled the *ſecondary* Law of *Nature*. The *primary* Law of *Nature*, according to the general Definition of it, is that which Nature has implanted in, and taught unto all living Creatures in common. As the Procreation of Children, and the Education of them, in Reſpect of Man, and the like; the Conjunction, or carnal Copulation of Male and Female in brute Beaſts; the Nurture of their Young, and the like: And this is (as I have ſaid before) properly called the *primary* Law of Nature. The *ſecondary* Law of Nature is the Law of right Reaſon, which accrues unto Mankind alone as the only Being upon Earth that has Reaſon for its Guide. Now the Law of Nature, as it is underſtood and taken in this Senſe, is that Knowledge and Conſent of Opinion, which is either naturally, or elſe by Divine Inſpiration, implanted and infus'd into the Minds of Men, touching the Duties of Morality and good Manners; and it propounds unto Mankind the best and most perfect Way of Life, by commanding those Things which ought to be done, and forbidding the contrary. This secondary Part, or Species of the Law of Nature, according to the Notion of some Persons, is acquir'd only from Nature it self; and being born with us, or imbib'd and stamp'd upon us at the Time of our first Being, is not learn'd by Reading, Education or Conversation; nor is it acquir'd by any Human Learning; all Men being by their Birth moulded and form'd hereunto. For the Law of Nature is that which is evident of it self, and wants no Demonstration, flowing from the first Principles of the Law of Nature, *viz.* That which is Good ought to be embraced, and that which is Evil avoided: But the Principles of the secondary Law of Nature are not so clear and evident of themselves: For a natural Law, in this Sense, may be given in such an obscure and unknown Manner, that we may, in some measure, be excus'd from the Transgression of it, by reason of invincible Ignorance, as already hinted.

And the same Thing may be said of first Principles. But the Definition of the Law of Nature, as given here, and in the first Book of the *Digests*, is commonly impugn'd, and improperly called the Law of Nature, because Brutes are not endued with Reason; and consequently, they can have no Law or Rule to govern and direct themselves; and therefore Brutes are not the proper Objects of Right, because they want Sense and Understanding to know and distinguish the same. So that that is pro-

properly called the Law of Nature, which Nature has taught and furnish'd out unto all Men, having its original Rise from God himself: And such is that which we call Religion towards God; Duty and Obedience towards our Parents; and a Love and Zeal for our Country, *&c.* Now all these Truths, or Principles, are contain'd in the Decalogue; and, in short, this Law comprehends this natural Precept of doing to another that which you have done unto your self. The Decalogue in the several Precepts therein contain'd shews us, what Kind of Knowledge this Law teaches us. 'Tis said, That *Justinian* has taken the Law of Nature in too large a Sense, and in a very gross Manner, when he uses it for a natural Inclination or Instinct; and that he ought rather to have defin'd and call'd it στοργας φυσικας, than the Law of Nature. But the Doctors endeavour to maintain this Definition; saying, That the Law of Nature is that which Nature has taught every living Creature *in suo genere*, that is to say, according to the Way and Manner that God has created every living Creature. For Brutes have a promiscuous Copulation or Conjunction with each other, according to their own proper Motion and Impulse, whereby or wherewith they are created, without any certain Kind of Reason, but by natural Instinct alone; for they do not understand, what is fit and decent to be done. But Man has a rational Judgment and Understanding, and ought to use and exercise the same. For he naturally knows and understands, that Comliness and Decency ought to be consider'd in the Copulation of Male and Female. Besides, in defence of this Definition the Doctors say, that this Definition ought to be understood of the *Primary*, and not of the *Secondary* Law of Nature, stiling the *Primary* Law of Nature, that which Men have in common with Brutes. And to this *Primary* Law of Nature this Definition is best adapted, since it only consists in Instinct and natural Inclination, and is common to Men, as well as other Animals. Such is the Love of Man's self, Self-Preservation, the avoiding of Things hurtful, and providing Things necessary for Life, the Procreation of our own Species, and the Care thereof, *&c.* The *Secondary* Law of Nature is that which is only fitted and adapted unto Man; and, this consisting in natural Reason only: It makes a Distinction between Mankind and all other Animals. Now the Effects and Consequences of the *Primary* Law of Nature are those two that follow, *viz.* *First*, The carnal Copulation of Man and Woman, or Male and Female. And, *Secondly*, The Procreation and Education of their Children, *&c.*

Cicero in the first Book of his Offices, says, That the Conjunction of Male and Female for the sake of Procreation, is an Appetite common unto all Animals; and so likewise is the Care and Nurture of their Off-spring implanted in them all by Nature. Altho' the Law of Nature is so far immutable and perpetual, that it cannot be weaken'd or taken away by any Human Law; yet it may receive and admit of some due Temperament and Qualification, if the Necessities of the State and Commonwealth do require the same; for, to promote the Peace and Tranquility thereof, it may be qualify'd by the Wisdom of the Civil Law. The

The Emperor *Justinian* reckons the Effects and Consequence of the Law of Nature to be two, *viz.* The Conjunction of Male and Female; And, *Secondly*, The Procreation and Education of Children, *&c.* as aforesaid. Touching the first of these in Respect of Man we find, that Matrimony was introduced by a manifold Law. *First*, By the Law of Nature in Respect of the Conjunction of Man and Woman. *Secondly*, By the Law of God in respect of its Institution and express Appointment; for God appointed Wedlock unto Man and Woman in *Paradise*; and from hence God is said to be the Author, Guardian, and President of Wedlock *, according to the *Canon* Law. *Thirdly*, By the Law of Nations, in respect of that Consent, whereby Matrimony is contracted; as all other Contracts, which are perfected by Consent, are said to be by the Law of Nations. And, *Fourthly*, By the Civil Law in respect of the Form and Solemnity of Matrimony, and the Prohibition of certain Marriages. But in the Decision of Matrimonial Causes, there are five Laws to be considered, *viz.* Custom before the Law of *Moses*. *Secondly*, The Law of *Moses* it self. *Thirdly*, The Civil Law of the *Romans*, the Law of the New Testament, and the *Canon* Law. The second Effect of the Law of Nature, is the Education of Children. Now touching this *Primary* Law of Nature it is said, that there is a natural Spur, which exhorts and incites us much to the Education of our Children. *Plutarch* observes, That Nature has therefore plac'd in the upper Part of a Woman's Body to shew, that an Infant ought to be treated with all Gentleness and Tenderness, Therefore Education,

* 32 Q. 4. 4.

in respect of natural Instinct, whereby Parents are mov'd to educate and maintain their Children, is founded on the Law of Nature; but in respect of Necessity, it is founded on the Civil Law. For by the *Civil* Law a Father may be compelled by the Office of the Judge to maintain his Children, according to the Measure of his Estate; and not only those that are under the Father's Power, and that are born in just Marriage, but also his emancipated Children, and those which are stiled *Naturales tantum.* And tho' Children born in Incest, and *ex damnato Coitu*, according to the Rigor of the Civil Law, are not to be maintain'd, yet by the Equity of the *Canon* Law, the Father is bound to maintain even these Children also. Whilst the Law of Nature was the Rule of Man's Life, Men sought for no larger Territories, than they themselves could compass and manure; they erected no other magnificent Buildings, than sufficient to defend them from Cold and Tempest; they cared for no other Delicacy of Fare, or Curiosity of Diet, than to maintain Life.

Of the Law of Nations.

HAving already explain'd the Law of Nature, before I proceed to speak of a positive Law, it will not be amiss to say something of the Law of Nations, so far as it relates to the Reason and Essence of a Law. *First*, Because

cauſe it has ſuch an Affinity with the Law of Nature, That ſeveral Perſons confound it with the Law of Nature, or (at leaſt) think it to be a certain Part of the Law of Nature. *Secondly*, Becauſe in the very Manner, as it is diſtinguiſh'd from the Law of Nature, it has a nearneſs of kin unto it; and is (as it were) a *Medium* between the Law of Nature, and a poſitive Law of Man; and is more nearly related to the former Extreme, than to the latter: And, therefore, by treating of the Law of Nations, here I ſhall make a more agreeable Tranſition to the Law of Man, properly ſo called, or (in other Terms) ſtiled the poſitive Law of Man.

That there is ſuch a Thing as the Law of Nations, all Perſons do agree in and ſuppoſe as a Thing certain and not to be doubted, even from the moſt frequent Uſe that our Law-Books make of this Expreſſion: For the *Civil* Law mentions it often, and ſo do's the *Canon* Law too. But becauſe this is an equivocal Expreſſion, we ought to diſtinguiſh it according to the proper Signification, wherein Lawyers only underſtand it. For the Word (*Jus*) ſometimes ſignifies a moral Power or Faculty, *ad rem aliquam vel in re aliquâ*: Whether it be true Dominion and Property, or only ſome Participation thereof, which is the proper Object of Juſtice. Sometimes the Word (*Jus*) ſignifies a Law, which is a Rule of Living, and doing that which is honeſt and virtuous; and, according to the former Senſe of the Word, is the Eſſence of the Law it ſelf; as it ordains and appoints a certain Degree of Equity in all human Affairs of Life: And as this Eſſence is the Law it ſelf, ſo the Word (*Jus*) is co-incident with the

Latin Word *Lex*. From whence we have these short Terms, which we make use of; calling the first *Jus honestum*, and the secoud *Jus utile*; or the first *Jus legale*, and the second *Jus reale*. Therefore each of them may be divided into the Law of Nature, the Law of Nations, and the Civil Law. For that is called, *Jus utile naturale*, when it is given by Nature it self, as flowing from it, and proceeding with it: And in this Sense, Liberty may be said to be deriv'd from the Law of Nature. That is called Civil Right, which the Civil Law introduces; as Prescription, Adoption, Emancipation, &c. And that is called, *Jus utile gentium*, or Right according to the Law of Nations, which was introduc'd by the Law of Nations. Now the Law of Nations is nothing else but the general Voice and Consent of Mankind introduc'd in respect of Persons, rendring some Men free, and other Men Vassals. It makes some to be *sui Juris*; and others do hereby become subject to the Power of a Father. Some Persons do hereby become Judges, and administer the Law unto others; and some admit of Jurisdiction to be exercis'd over them. Now this Law of Nations is not subject to the Power of Princes: And for this Reason, the Law of Nations can neither be abrogated nor repeal'd by the Prince, nor by the Force of Custom in a State; because it was introduc'd by and founded on natural Reason. And tho' God has subjected all other human Institutions to the Power of Princes and Sovereign States; yet he has not made the Law of Nations subject thereunto. It was by this Law of Nations, that the Division of Things was found out and introduc'd troduc'd among Men, as *Meum* and *Tuum* was. And from hence, Diſtinct Kingdoms and ſeparate Properties aroſe among Princes: The diſtinct Dominions and Territories of Kingdoms being entirely owing to the Law of Nations. For the Preſervation of Men and Things, ſays a great Author, theſe two great Luminaries were here appointed upon Earth, *viz. Magiſtracy* and the *Prieſthood*, in *Latin* called *Imperium* and *Sacerdotium*, after the Manner of thoſe two great Lights in the Heavens; and their Offices are diſtinct and ſeparate.

The Law of Nations is of much larger Extent and Juriſdiction than the Civil Law, as deriving its Authority from the joint Conſent of all Men, or (at leaſt) from the Concurrence of moſt Nations in the World: I ſay, *of moſt Nations*; becauſe there is ſcarce any Law beſides that of Nature (which is even ſometimes ſtiled the Law of Nations) that is common to all Nations. Yea, what is reckon'd the Law of Nations in one Part of the World, is not accounted ſuch in another Part thereof, As I ſhall ſhew in ſpeaking of Captivity and *Poſtliminy*. The Law of Nations is prov'd after the ſame Manner as the unwritten Civil Law is, *viz.* By continual Uſage, and the Teſtimony of Men ſkilful in Hiſtory, and the Laws themſelves: The Law of Nations being the Daughter of Time, and a well gather'd Experience. And to this end, are the Annals of former Ages of ſingular Uſe and Advântage.

It has been ſaid, that the Law of Nations is that Law, which natural Reaſon has ordain'd and enacted almoſt among all Nations. And by this Law Wars were firſt introduc'd, and diſtinct

stinct Nations and Kingdoms were erected, and Lands set out with Metes and Bounds unto Men. Nor were these Things alone the only Product of the Law of Nations; but this Law also introduc'd the Building of Houses, Commerce, Manumissions, and the Institution of all Obligations: Except those few, which were afterwards introduc'd by the Civil Law. And this in a strict Sense is properly called the Law of Nations, which otherwise in a more extended Acceptation is stiled the Law of Nature it self: And hence it is, that the Doctors have distinguish'd it into the *Primary* and *Secondary* Law of Nations. For the Law of Nations is divided into two Species or Parts, as the Law of Nature it self is. The first is stiled the *Primary* Law of Nations; and is that Law, which was introduc'd by natural Reason at that very Time, when Nations, or rather Mankind it self began to have a first Being without any formal Constitution, or enacting Power among Men. And properly speaking, this is nothing else, but the *Secondary* Law of Nature, or such Ideas and Notions, as God himself has imprinted on the Minds of Men; and by these Ideas and Notions our natural Reason judges and determines for us, what is decent and fit to be done: And in this Sense, Religion towards God proceeds from the Law of Nations. Indeed some Persons have disputed, whether this Religion be a Matter of publick Right; that is to say, whether it belongs to the *Jus Publicum* or not; because according to them it is a Sacrament. But I can see no Reason, why it should admit of any Dispute. For since God do's not stand in need of our good Works, I can-

cannot learn of what Advantage this Diſpute can be to any one; it being our own private Intereſt to fear God and reverence the Deity. Nor is this Religion towards God a Sacrament then, but it is the Force of Reaſon radicated in Mankind by Nature it ſelf, and is even common to the *Gentiles*, who have no ſuch Things as Sacraments. From whence the Poet *Statius* ſays, *Primus in orbe Deos Timor fecit.*

The Second Part or *Species* is that which we call the *Secondary* Law of Nations. And this is that Law, which all Nations and States make Uſe of, from its being conſtituted and made into a Law. And tho' it proceeds from a Kind of natural Judgment; yet it was not ſimply ſo from the beginning, but was afterwards conſtituted, and had its Being from the common Uſage of all Mankind, and from human Neceſſities requiring the ſame. And this is properly called the Law of Nations, which I have here defin'd to be that common Uſage and Cuſtom, which is receiv'd among Men, in order to diſtinguiſh it from the *proper* Law of Nature. Now this *Secondary* Law of Nations, ſometimes recedes and eſtranges it ſelf from the proper Law of Nature; and do's in ſome Meaſure detract from it by introducing Services and Vaſſalage: And ſometimes it adds thereunto in diſcovering *de novo* the Properties of Things. And 'tis to be obſerv'd, that the Law of Nations in our Law-Books is ſometimes taken for the true and proper Law of Nature, and ſometimes for that Law, which is common unto all Mankind, either from a general Obſervation thereof, or elſe from ſome kind of Conſtitution and Uſage, for that it is observ'd among all Nations as a Law. And sometimes the Law of Nature is put for the Law of Nations: For the Law of Nature, as it is proper to the Nature of Man, is the Law of right Reason; which in respect of the Effect and Use of it, is also called the Law of Nations. And it is also stiled the *Common Law*, whenever it is propounded and made the peculiar Law of any State or Commonwealth. Altho' this seems proper to the Civil Law; yet in this respect the *Secondary* Law of Nations agrees with the Civil Law, *viz.* That both of them do not in all Things agree with natural Reason, but either adds or detracts something from it. But herein it differs, *viz.* For that the *Secondary* Law of Nations is constituted and observ'd almost by all Nations, and is founded upon a kind of Ratiocination, according to the Exigencies of human Necessities; but the Civil Law is only constituted and ordain'd in that, or this particular State or Commonwealth so requiring it. Moreover, the Civil Law not only sometimes recedes from the Law of Nature, but also from the Law of Nations. For by the Law of Nations all Trade and Commerce are free, but by the Civil Law or by a Municipal Statute, the Exportation of Corn, Wine, Oyl, *&c.* may be prohibited; the Necessity of the State or Commonwealth requiring the same.

The good Effects and Consequences of the Law of Nations, was Religion towards God: I mean a certain kind of Reverence and Worship paid him, whereby the Mind of Man has determin'd God to be an Omnipotent Creator and Preserver of all Things, and a Benefactor to juſt and righteous Men, and a Puniſher of evil Doers. And for this Reaſon it is, That the Mind of Man judges God to be fear'd, worſhipped, and called upon. For tho' the Knowledge of the Divine Law be obſcur'd much by original Sin, yet it is not wholly extinguiſh'd. For as *Cicero* obſerves in his *Tuſculan* Queſtions, *There is no Nation ſo fierce and bruitiſh, and no People ſo ſavage, but that they have their Minds ſeaſon'd and endued with an Opinion and Belief of a God.* Indeed, there are many, that conceive and entertain evil Thoughts of the Divine Majeſty through a vicious Courſe of Thinking and Living; yet they all acknowledge ſome Divine Power and Nature exiſting. And again in his Second Book of the Nature of the Gods, he expreſly ſays, That the Being of a God is innate unto all Men, and is a Part of Knowledge engraven on the Minds of Men: So that according to him the Being of a God is an innate Principle, and an Idea impreſs'd (as it were) on the Mind of Man.

The Second good Effect of the Law of Nations, is a filial Piety and Duty towards our Parents, and a Love and Zeal for our Country; that is to ſay, a due and proper Obedience to our Parents, and a Submiſſion unto the Laws and Welfare of our Country. And hence it is, that *Ulpian* ſays, That a Son, who uſes any Contumely towards his Father and Mother, whom he ought to honour and reverence, ſhall be ſeverely puniſh'd; for the Perſon of the Parent ought to be held with the Son, as *Res ſancta & honeſta.* Yet we ought rather to obey our Father than our Mother*, where they command Things indifferent in their

* D. 1. 1. 2. l. 5. 4. 8.

their own Nature; and the Power of the Father
*I. ii. 10. infers this, which Power is not in the Mother *, as being the weaker Vessel. Here the Doctors put a Case, *viz.* That if a *Filius-famil* has let himself out to Hire, to work for some Artificer for a Time certain, and has promis'd not to depart from him within that Time, and yet notwithstanding the Father calls him Home. *Quere*, Whether he ought rather to obey his Father's Command, than keep his Promise? And by what I have said before, He ought rather to obey his Father, since this Obedience arises from the Law of Nations. But *Albericus*, as quoted by *Claudius*, decides it on the contrary, namely, That we ought not to contravene our Contract, when we have once made one; For a Contract is also founded on the Law of Nations, as well as filial Obedience: And this (I think) is a right Opinion, it being *Fomentum fidei servandæ*. And this makes for what is commonly said, *viz.* That a *Filius-famil*, or a Person under the Power of a Father, may be as well oblig'd by his Con-
† D. 5. 1. tract, as by any Offence he shall commit †;
5 7. 29. 2. And such a Son may be imprison'd, till such
92. Time as he performs his Covenant ‖.

‖ D. 4. 4. By the Law of Nations 'tis said; That we
3. 3. ought to shew a Love and Zeal for our Country, and yield a due Obedience unto its Laws, and an entire Submission to its Interest and Welfare; because we are born to do it Ser-
* D. 25. 5. vice *. Whence it happens, That if a Citizen
1. or Subject shall not assist and help the State or Commonwealth whereunto he belongs, when the same is in Danger, he shall lose the Right of a Denizon, and the Privileges given him by his

his Country *. And as a Son, that leaves his Father in Danger, or do's not point out an imminent Danger to him, may be puniſh'd as a Parricide: So may a Perſon be puniſh'd, that deſerts and forſakes the Intereſt of his Country. Hence it is, That Traytors and other Impugners of its Welfare, do incur the Crime and Puniſhment of High-Treaſon: For we are not born for our ſelves and Parents alone, but for the Good of our Country alſo. For tho' our Parents, Children and familiar Acquaintance are dear to every one of us; yet our Country commands us the greateſt Love of all; and we ought rather to obey our Country than our Parents, if we cannot comply with them both. So that a Son may even kill his Father, that comes with a Purpoſe and Reſolution of deſtroying his Country. Theſe are the Effects of the *Primary* Law of Nations.

* *Bald. in* l. 2. *Tit.* 52. lib. 8. *Cod.*

By the *Secondary* Law of Nations, Wars were introduc'd for the Puniſhment of the Guilty, and for the mutual Defence of Men's Perſons and Properties. For this Conſtitution about making Wars, had not its Riſe and Beginning at the ſame Time with Mankind it ſelf, but was introduc'd after the Diſtinction of Property, and the Dominion of Things began to prevail among Men: And when this Dominion and Property began to be invaded thro' the deprav'd Corruption of Men's Manners, it was produc'd for the Preſervation of human Society and common Peace among Mankind. And this is ſtrictly called the Law of Nations, but in a larger Senſe it is taken for the Law of Nature it ſelf. And from hence the Doctors have diſtinguiſh'd it into the *Primary* and *Secondary* Law of Nations.

Now

Of the Civil Law in general.

Now a Kingdom, State or Commonwealth are all of them included under the *Latin* Word *Civitas*, and each of these is a compleat Number of Freemen associated together for the Defence of their own Rights, and for the mutual Help and Advantage of each other. The Civil Law in this Sense (I say) is that Law, which every distinct State or Commonwealth has ordain'd for its own peculiar Use and Service, according to that Majesty and Severeign Power with which every Kingdom, State and Commonwealth is vested: And this is neither intirely distinct from the Law of Nature, nor is it subservient thereunto in all Respects; but it either adds or detracts something from the Secondary Law of Nature. Now the Civil Law, in this Sense, is either a written or an unwritten Law. I call that a written Law, where the Mind and Will of the Law-giver is in express Terms committed to Writing, because most Nations and Commonwealths do usually reduce their Laws into Writing; tho' Writing be not necessary to the Substance of a Law.

The End of the Civil Law in the Extent of its Signification is the Preservation of Man, as he is born a Political Animal, and is a Member of human Society within this or that Commonwealth; directing his Actions to a happy State or Way of Living; or it is ordain'd for the good Government of a certain Number of Men in some particular State or Commonwealth; and it matters not, whether this be the Civil Law of the *Romans*, or of any other State. Therefore the End of the Civil Law may be said to be a certain kind of Friendship, as it were, according to which *Aristotle* in the first

firſt Book of his *Ethicks* deſcribes it to to be the good Government, and well ordering of Civil Society. For a Commonwealth or State is nothing elſe but a Multitude of Perſons collected and gather'd together, with a proper and ſufficient Power to maintain and defend the State of their Goods and Properties; ſuch Society being link'd and join'd together by an agreeable Obligation of Laws, and by a common Way of Life. But the end of the *Canon* Law under a good Regulation is of a more excellent Uſe and Nature, than that of the Civil Law of a State; it being for the Defence and Preſervation of Man, as he is a Chriſtian, and expects another Life after this, which is eternal in the Heavens: And this Law not only relates to human Friendſhip in this preſent Life, but it alſo concerns that heavenly Fellowſhip which we ſhall have with God, and each other in the World to come; not by making of us Denizons of *Rome*, *Venice* or any other State and Commonwealth, but Citizens of the heavenly *Jeruſalem*, according to what the Scriptures ſay *.

The Civil Law in general is not the ſame in all Nations and Commonwealths, but it varies and changes in ſeveral States, and is in a different Manner peculiar to each reſpective Country or Nation: And this Law is ſo immediately deriv'd to them by the Law of Nature, as the Law of Nations is. For it is partly deduc'd from ſuch Principles as all Nations do not agree in or readily aſſent to; becauſe they depend on particular Circumſtances, which are various, and in no wiſe adapted to all States and Nations. Wherefore *Ulpian* ſays *, That the Civil Law neither wholly differs from the

* Heb. 12. 22.

* In *l.* 6. *D. Tit. de Juſt.* &c.

the Law of Nature and Nations, nor is it in all Points conformable thereunto. Therefore, when we add any Thing thereunto, or take any Thing away from the Law which is common to all Men, we make a Law which is proper and peculiar unto our own State, and this is called the Civil Law of our own Country in the extended Signification of the Words. And in this Acceptation the Constitutions of a Province or Kingdom are stiled the Civil Law in respect of such Province or Kingdom: As it is said of the Constitutions of the Kingdom of *Naples*, *Germany*, *France*, and the like. Tho' the *Feudal* Law be a customary Law, yet it may notwithstanding properly enough be stiled the Civil Law; and in this Sense the Law of the *Lombards* is the Civil Law of *Lombardy*, because it was made by Kings and Emperors, as other Laws were. For the *Lombards*, that first came out of *Germany* into *Sardinia*, and then passed out of *Sardinia* into *Apulia*, had their Kings equally with other civiliz'd Nations.

Tho' a Civil or Municipal Law can enjoin nothing, that the Law of Nature or Nations forbids; nor forbid any Thing, which the Law of Nature or Nations enjoins; yet it may notwithstanding limit and circumscribe that, which the Law of Nature or Nations has left free, and forbid that which is lawful to be done in a State of Nature. And in this Manner the Civil Law may by interposing its Authority, prevent and hinder that Dominion and Property, which is acquir'd by the Law of Nature, and purchas'd by the Law of Nations: So that human Laws may command Things which are preternatural, but can ordain nothing

thing that is contrary to Nature. The Law of Nature and of Nations obtains in all States and in all Cases, wherein the Civil Law cannot be practis'd and executed; as betwixt foreign Princes, and the like. And where the Law of Nature and of Nations is violated and infring'd, every Prince may make War on the Violator thereof. And here I make Use of the Law of Nature and of Nations, to denote one and the same Thing differently express'd.

In a doubtful Case, when we meet with these Words, *viz. The Civil Law*, we thereby mean the Common Civil Law of the *Romans*; that is to say, when these Words are express'd in *unâ Specie* alone; then I say, they are intended to be understood of the Civil Law as common to the *Romans*. But if they are express'd *simply* and *absolutely* in the following Manner, *viz. de Jure*, or *de Jure Civili*; then they are design'd to be taken *de omni Jure*, and to be understood of the Civil Law in general, as I have been discoursing of it; because an *infinite* Term is equivalent to an *Universal*.

Now since the Civil or Municipal Law of any Nation, is only to be acquir'd by much Study; which is an earnest and vehement Application of the Mind to do something that is painful and laborious to accomplish; let none hope to attain the Knowledge of the Civil Law without an earnest and vehement Application of Mind and Thought. For Skill and Knowledge in the Laws is produc'd and gotten by a deep Search into many Things, since a Lawyer ought not only to have a Knowledge of the whole Civil Law, this being the first Thing; but he ought also to understand Philosophy, especially *Ethicks*, *Logick*, Oratory, and particularly the Propriety of the *Latin* Tongue, if he designs to make himself a good Proficient in the *Roman* Law. And of these Things he ought to have a full and perfect Knowledge, which has been wanting in several Men (otherwise not without Learning) in ancient as well as modern Times.

Publick Laws are Matters of publick Benefit and Advantage; and private Laws do only relate to private Men in their private Capacity and State of Life, betwixt which there intervenes the Law of Nature, of which I shall treat by and by. There is one Kind of Law which is Publick, and another which is Private. The first of these is that which has a principal Regard to the Advantage of the publick State or Commonwealth; and the latter is that which chiefly regards the Affairs of private Men; but it is to be observ'd, that the private is included in the publick Law. For who do's not know, that Priests and Magistrates are for the Advantage of each particular Man, if they act as they ought to do? Thus on the contrary, do's not the private Law contain in it self the publick Law? For tho' Trade and Commerce, and the having of rich Subjects, be a Matter relating to the *Jus privatum*; yet as this increases private Mens Estates, it also enriches the Publick, and becomes a National Advantage; and consequently may in some Measure seem to come under the *Jus publicum*.

The Study of the Law consists of two Parts, namely, that of the *Jus publicum*, which relates to the State of the *Roman*, or any other Common-

wealth;

wealth; and that of the *Jus privatum*, which respects the Advantage of particular Men only. Now these Things herein differ, since the publick Law is deriv'd from nothing else but from the Precepts of Nature, the Law of Nations and the Civil Law. And as a Municipal Law is ordain'd and constituted for the Use and Advantage of the *Roman* Commonwealth, so it is called *Jus Publicum*: For the Law is not stiled *Jus Publicum* in respect of its Form, that is to say, because it was publickly ordain'd and constituted; but in respect of its Object and End, because it relates to the Priesthood, to Things sacred, to Magistrates, and to the Government of other publick Matters. That which is called a *private written Law*, is that which every State or Commonwealth enacts and ordains for its own peculiar Use, with the express Consent of the People; and this is said in some Measure to be a Law proper and peculiar to such a State or Commonwealth; and in other Terms it is stiled the Statute or Municipal Law thereof; as the *Roman* Civil Law, or the Statute Law of *England* is. I have said in this Definition with *the express Consent of the People*, to distinguish it from Custom; because Custom is introduc'd by the tacit Consent of the People alone. For the Explication of this Subject concerning Statutes, I shall first observe, That every City or Corporation, that is to say, every Communion and Body Politick, may regularly make Statutes to bind its own People, or Inhabitants. But then it ought to be with this Distinction, *viz*. For either the People have the whole Jurisdiction granted them from the Prince; or else they have it by

Prescription, and then they may make Decrees and Statutes for the Decision of Causes without the Confirmation and Authority of the Prince, or any other superior Power, by the Permission of the Law alone. Or else, *Secondly*, The People have only a limited Jurisdiction, as in Civil Causes only, or in Criminal Causes of a light and slender Nature; and then they can only do this in Matters, whereof they have full Jurisdiction. For in other Cases they cannot make Decrees and Ordinances, without the Confirmation and Authority of their Superior. Or else, *Thirdly*, The People have no Jurisdiction at all, as in Villes and Castellanies that are in Subjection to some City or Lord thereof: And in this Case, it is not lawful for them to make Decrees and Ordinances for the Decision of Causes, unless they be confirm'd by the Sovereign Authority. Thus in the last Law of the Code, *touching Last-Wills and Testaments*, the Custom of *Rusticks* is held as valid in respect of Testaments and making Last-Wills, because the Prince or Emperor has confirm'd the same. But in respect of the Administration of Goods, they may make Decrees and Orders about the common Expence of Money, without any such special Authority, unless these Orders and Decrees do favour too much of Ambition.

But the Law now commonly called the *Civil Law* had its Birth in *Rome*; and was written by the *Decemviri* about three Hundred Years after the first Foundation of the City: And it was compiled not only out of the ancient *Roman* Customs, and the Laws of their Kings, but also from the *Athenian* and other *Grecian* Laws.

Laws. The Regal Laws being devised and enacted by their first Kings, were in *Latin* stiled *Leges Regiæ*, and *Leges Papyrianæ*; the last, because they were collected by *Papyrius* in the Reign of *Tarquin*, as I shall hereafter remember. For though, as many of the former Laws as maintain'd kingly Government and Authority, were abolish'd with the Name of a King, yet those of *Servius Tullius* made on the Account of Commerce and Contracts, and all such as appertain'd to Religion, and the common Utility of the State, were continued and made Part of the Law of the Twelve Tables. To these Laws of the Twelve Tables in Process of Time were added (as the Business of the State gave Occasion) those Laws made by the Senate, and in *Latin* called *Senatus Consulta*; and likewise of the common People, in *Latin* stiled *Plebiscita*. And, *Thirdly*, Those of the Lawyers named *Responsa Prudenta*. The Edicts of the yearly Magistrate, commonly called a *Prætor*, made another Part of the old *Roman* Law: But these Edicts, as they were at first only of yearly Continuance, after they had been collected and interpreted by *Julian*, and presented by him to the Emperor *Adrian*, were by the said Emperor confirm'd, and made perpetual Laws, under the Title of the *Perpetual* Edict: As I shall have Occasion to observe more at large hereafter in my Treatise of the *Roman* Laws. The ancient Difference betwixt *Laws* and *Edicts*, by the *French* stiled *Reglements*, consisted herein, *viz*. That Laws are the Constitutions made or confirmed by Sovereign Authority (be it placed in one, in few, or in the People) and are also general and permanent: But an Edict (which is but *Jussum Magistratus*, unless it be made a Law by due Authority) has an end with the Magistrate or Officer himself, who made the same. And, according to *Varro*, they who ascribe the most to an Edict, affirm it to be a Law but for one Year only. *Isidore*, by *Edicts* and *Constitutions* indeed understands those Acts of Prerogative, sometimes called *Ordinances*: As an Ordinance or Edict is that which a King or Emperor ordains and proclaims by the Advice of his Privy Council.

Whenever there is any general mention made of the Law in our Books, the *Civil Law* of the *Romans* is intended thereby, which is divided into a *written* and *unwritten* Law; the one being called the *Law in general*, and the other stiled *Custom*. Now *Custom* or the *unwritten Civil Law* of the *Romans*, was that Law which Custom and immemorial Usage had approv'd of, and which the *tacit* Consent of the People had introduc'd among them. This was also stiled *Length of Custom*, and *Diuturnity of Practice*; because such a frequent Repetition of Acts, and such a length of Time was requir'd to introduce this kind of Law, as is sufficient to prove the tacit Consent of the Peoples Readiness to receive the same. And thus Custom rightly introduc'd imitates a *written Law*: That is to say, it has the same Force and Authority, as such a Law has. For it matters not, whether the People declare this their Consent and Choice, either by their own express Suffrage, or else by Things and Acts themselves that are equivalent unto Suffrage. But then it must be acknowledg'd, that this kind of Law

chief-

chiefly belongs unto a free State and People, that is vested with Majesty and Sovereign Power, for the Reasons already mention'd: For a People under an absolute Subjection to a Prince cannot introduce an *unwritten* Law without the Presumption, Consent and Approbation of the Prince, at least. Of the *written Civil Law* of the *Romans* I shall speak hereafter more at large.

CHAPTER *the Third.*

Of LAWS *in General.*

THERE are several Things here to be inquir'd into in general. *First*, What Laws may be chang'd and alter'd? *Secondly*, Who has the Power of changing and altering Laws? *Thirdly*, After what Manner they may be chang'd and alter'd, and by what Methods. And, *Fourthly*, Who has the Power of expounding Laws, and how Laws ought to be expounded. *First*, It appears, That the Laws of Nature, which are in a like manner observed among all People and Nations, are immutable (as I have already remark'd) because they flow, and are deriv'd from a certain kind of eternal Truth or Law; but Civil Laws may freely, and without Restraint, be chang'd and abrogated, according to the Advantage and Necessity of every Estate or Kingdom. A Civil Law is nothing else but an Affirmation of the Law of Nature, or of Natural Right; and it being always

ways referr'd *ad rationem Naturæ*, it may be chang'd; for sometimes Civil Laws recede a great way from natural Reason, but then they ought to ordain nothing that savours of Iniquity. The Civil Law being a Determination of the Law of Nature, and the Law of Nations, it has a Respect unto Civil Philosophy, or Civil Polity; and may be chang'd two several Ways, as I shall observe by and by. *Secondly*, The Power of abrogating and changing Laws is lodg'd in the Hands of them that have the Right and Power of making Laws: And these Persons are of a twofold Kind and Nature. *First*, A State or Commonwealth, that is not absolutely govern'd by any single Person, called a Monarch, may make Laws and Constitutions for themselves. And, *Secondly*, The Prince, whether he be only such an one as represents the People in a mix'd Government, or if he be an absolute and despotick Prince, may do it. Thus no Law or Custom in *England* can be repealed or abrogated, unless it be by the Authority of Parliament, which has the Power of making Laws. *Thirdly*, This Change of Laws may be wrought and effected either by some other Law made, or else by a tacit Consent of the People, which is by a Disuser thereof, and not by a Non-user only; but it must be done by a contrary Use and Practice (as some will have it) shewing the Mind and Inclination of the People leading hereunto. But that Law, which has been once reduc'd into Writing, cannot afterwards be chang'd without some express repealing Law; yet a Law in Writing is not immediately taken for a Law certainly ordained and enacted, since it requires a subsequent Promulgation.

Touch-

Touching the Explanation of Laws, it is firſt to be obſerv'd, That the Law muſt be aided and ſupply'd by Interpretation: And the Law provides, That it ſhall be in his Power to interpret a Law, in whoſe Power it was to make or ordain the ſame. Now the ſeveral Species of interpreting Laws are Four in Number, *viz.* *Firſt*, The Interpretation of the Prince, or Sovereign Power, is ſaid to be a general Interpretation, becauſe it is extended unto all Perſons. *Secondly*, It is ſaid to be *neceſſary*, becauſe we are neceſſarily oblig'd to follow the ſame: And ſuch an Interpretation ought to be reduc'd into Writing, becauſe ſome Lawyers will have it, that all Laws ought to be reduc'd into Writing; Writing, according to them, being the Subſtance of a Law or Statute: And this kind of Interpretation being deem'd as a Law, it ought certainly to be reduc'd into Writing. But the common Opinion ſeems to be, That Writing is not the Subſtance of a Law; for the Reducing of a Law into Writing, is only for the ſake of preſerving the Memory thereof. And for this Opinion we have a good Text in the Law, ſaying, That when a Succeſſor reduces any Conſtitution of his Predeceſſors into Writing, he does it that it may not be loſt; it being otherwiſe ſubject unto Oblivion. Therefore, if the Conſtitution it ſelf was valid, before it was reduc'd into Writing; the Writing in ſuch a Caſe, where it intervenes after the Making of the Law, does not reſpect the Validity of ſuch a Law, but only helps to preſerve the Memory of it. According to the *Civil* Law the Prince's Pleaſure has the Force and Vigor of a Law; and therefore the Will and Pleaſure of the Prince alone effectually makes and

and establishes a Law without Writing. *Secondly*, There is another *Species* of interpreting a Law which is made by Custom; and Custom is the best Interpreter of Laws. Now this *Species* of Interpretation is *general*, as being extended to all Persons and Places where such Custom prevails; and it is also stiled *necessary* after the aforesaid Manner, because we are oblig'd to follow the same: Yet it is not reduc'd into Writing, because Custom subsists by Human Memory alone. The *Third Species* of Interpretation is that which is made by the Judge, being stiled a *judicial* Interpretation: For the Judge of a Cause may, in doubtful Matters, expound and interpret Laws in Relation to such Causes as are decided by his Sentence. And this *Species* of Interpretation is not *general*, because other Judges are not bound to pronounce Judgment according to a Precedent founded on his Sentence: For they ought to judge according to the Laws, and not according to Precedents. Yet this *Species* of Interpretation is also term'd *necessary*, because the Parties in Judgment are necessarily oblig'd to yield Obedience thereunto, and to observe the same. And this *Species* of Interpretation, in respect of the Judges definitive Sentence, ought to be reduc'd into Writing. The *Fourth Species* of Interpretation is that which is made by some Master or Doctor of Law; for every Master, or Doctor, may interpret doubtful Matters, or Points of Law, as arising within his own Faculty, wherein he has, or (at least) ought to have a thorough Learning and Experience. And this Interpretation of the Doctors is neither *general, necessary*, nor need it to be reduc'd into Writing: For the Interpretation

terpretation of a Doctor does not neceſſarily bind us to follow the ſame, but we only ſo far rely on it, as Law and Reaſon approves thereof.

An Interpretation ought always to be made in ſuch a manner, as not to render the Act or Law it ſelf eluſory. An Interpretation of Law ceaſes, when the Will and Intention of the Legiſlator clearly appears: And, in a doubtful Caſe, an Interpretation ought rather to be made for the Validity of the Act or Matter interpreted, than for the Invalidity and Deſtroying thereof. Sometimes a Matter is interpreted in a large Senſe, as in Contracts; ſometimes in a large Senſe, as in laſt Wills and Teſtaments: And ſometimes in the largeſt Senſe, as in reſpect of defamatory Words. When I ſay the *largeſt Senſe*, I mean the moſt favourable. But a Privilege ought not to be interpreted in a large Senſe, becauſe it is contrary to the Common Law, and concerns the Right of another Perſon. By the Papal Canon Law, in all Matters of a Spiritual or Eccleſiaſtical Nature, Recourſe ought to be had to the Pope for the Interpretation of Reſcripts and Privileges in doubtful Caſes *, which brings great Profit, and is a * X. 2. mighty Support to the Papacy. When a Law is 1. 12. made in favour of any one, it ought never to be interpreted in Hatred and Prejudice of him. Nor ought we to adhere to the *Cortex* and Outſide of the Law, but to the Senſe and internal Meaning thereof. Interpreters of Laws do make Laws by their Interpretation thereof. A prohibitory Law, that is to ſay, a Law which forbids any Thing to be done, is not reſtrain'd to the very Caſe expreſs'd therein, for it reaches to all Caſes of the like Nature; and conſequent-

ly

ly by this means, ſuch a Law receives an extenſive Interpretation.

Now every Law conſiſts, and is made up of two Things †. *Firſt*, It conſiſts, and is made up of the Words whereby ſuch a Law is expreſſed and declar'd. And, *Secondly*, It conſiſts, and is made up of the Senſe and Meaning of ſuch Law. The Words of a Law are either thoſe Signs and Characters wherein a Law is penn'd and written, and by means of which the Law it ſelf is convey'd to our Minds and Underſtandings. And the Senſe and Meaning of a Law is the Mind and Intention of the Legiſlator himſelf ‖: That is to ſay, That which the Law intends, and would have done, or not have done. And this is a certain Tenet and Maxim in all Laws, That whenever the Words of a Law differ from the Deſign and Intention of it, we ought only to follow the Deſign and Intention of ſuch a Law *. And this our Common Law Judges have obſerved in the Expoſition of ſeveral Statutes.

† D. 1. 3. 29. D. 50. 16 6.

‖ D. 1. 3. 30. & 32. C. 1. 14. 5.

* D. 1. 3. 17.

Now the Senſe and Meaning of a Law, which in other Terms I call the Intention of it, may be found and known to differ from the Words of it two ſeveral Ways. *Firſt*, If the Senſe and Meaning thereof be more limited and reſtrain'd than the Words themſelves couch'd under ſuch a Law. *Secondly*, When the Deſign and Intention of ſuch a Law is of a larger Extent than the Words themſelves will properly bear. And theſe two, in other Terms, we call a reſtrictive and an extenſive Interpretation. The Senſe and Meaning of a Law may be diſcover'd to be more limited and reſtrain'd than the Words thereof, four ſeveral Ways. *Firſt*, By ſome Exception mention'd and ſpecify'd in the ſame Law: As when

when a Precedent, or subsequent Exception, does qualify, govern and moderate something that is more general in such a Law†. *Secondly*, It may be discover'd from the Reason given and made use of in such a Law; for if the Reason of the Law ceases, the Law immediately ceases and comes to an end; there being no further Occasion of it‖. *Thirdly*, It may be discovered from the Equity thereof, and this Equity ought to be the chief Reason and Essence of every Law*. *Fourthly*, If there be a Law which is written in very general Terms, it governs other Laws, wherein there are special Exceptions.

† D. 12 1. 20.

‖ D. 1. 14. 32.

* C. 3. 1. 8. D. 1. 3 18. D 41. 9. 12.

The Meaning and Intention of a Law is known to be of a larger Extent than the Words themselves, Three several Ways, *viz. First, Ex contrario* (as we say) *viz.* When in a contrary Matter, the contrary of that, which is enacted and ordain'd, is understood to be intended by the Law†. *Secondly, Ex consequenti* (as we phrase it) namely, When a Law forbids that which follows upon some certain Points therein laid down and enacted. *Thirdly*, By way of Interpretation, as when we proceed to Consequences in those Things wherein there is the same, or else a Parity of Reason‖: Provided always, there be nothing introduc'd by these three Ways which is contrary to the Common Law*. The Law is extended to similar Cases, either by the Interpretation of a private Man, where the Reason thereof lays the Matter open and clear; or else, by the Prince's Constitution, where the Reason thereof is dark and obscure†. But what I have noted here ought only to be observ'd when it evidently appears, That the Intention of the Laws differs from the Words thereof. But in a doubt-

† D. 50. 17. 30. *& seq.* C. 1. 14. 5.

‖ D. 1. 3. 12. *& seq.* 11.

* D. 1. 3. 14. *& seq.*

† D. 1. 3. 12. *& seq.*

doubtful Case it is far better to observe and ad-
|| D. 14. 1. 1. 20. here to the Words themselves||.

But, What if the whole Sentence be dark and obscure in it self; and by this means the Design and Intention of the Law becomes obscure? Now such an Obscurity either consists in an Ambiguity of each particular Word; or else in the Construction of the whole Sentence it self, where there are indeed two Sentences; or else, *Lastly*, It consists in an Uncertainty of Things or Persons: Therefore all Rules of Law which treat of Interpretation are adapted hereunto. In this Case we ought, *First* of all, To consider what Things go before, and what are subsequent thereunto* *Secondly*, That what is express'd be utter'd and declar'd *sine vitio*; that is to say, without Flaw or Impropriety of Speech†. *Thirdly*, We ought to have a Recourse to Custom and former Laws, which is the best Interpreter of all Laws||. And, *Fourthly*, In doubtful Matters we ought to prefer the more benign and better Meaning to that which is less so*. For, *First*, We ought not to leave the true and genuine Signification of Words, or to depart from thence, unless it evidently appears, That the Writer took them in another Sense.

* D. 1. 3. 24.

† D. 1. 3. 19.

|| D. 1. 3. 35. & 37.

* D. 30. 14. 56.

It is a general Rule in Law, and that a very true one too, That wheresoever there is an Enumeration of Particulars of several Ranks and Degrees, beginning with the higher, and ending with the lower; and in the close, a general Expression of others *is added and joined with them:* Those others must not be understood to be a higher Rank, and superior Degree, to that which is last mention'd in the Law, but must be either of the same Degree or a lower†. But

† *Coke* 2. Rep. p. 46.

if

if the Enumeration goes upwards, beginning with a lower, and rising to a higher Degree; as if it be said, *Barons, Earls,* and *other Peers,* here Marquisses and Dukes will be comprehended; for the Case is then otherwise. A Law or favourable Statute ought to be extended to a Case of the like Nature, tho' such Law or Statute shou'd say, that such an Extension shall not be made. A new Law may be extended *ad præterita Pendentia,* when this is expresly provided, and taken Care of therein. A Law seems an Act, tho' it do's not forbid it expresly, but when it orders it to be with a certain kind of Solemnity; as that a Minor shou'd not make a Contract, *sine Consanguineis.* A Law ought always to be restrain'd and extended to prevent any Inhumanity ensuing thereon. When the Law requires a qualify'd Act, 'tis not enough to prove that Act without a Quality annex'd to it. Every Man is presum'd to know the Laws of his own Country either himself, or else by the Means of some other Person unto whom as a Counsellor learned in the Laws, he ought to apply himself. For after Laws are made and promulgated, a Presumption arises that they are known unto all Persons that are obliged to know the same: And therefore we say, that every Person is presum'd to know the Laws and Constitutions that do oblige him. And not a bare Knowledge of the Promulgation of a Law is presum'd, but a Man is even presum'd to know the Orders and Disposition of the Law. And that which we say of all common Laws in general, may be also said of Statutes and Municipal Laws; for even these are presum'd to be known by the Citizens, after they have been publish'd. This Presumption is also extended to have Place, even in an unwritten Law, that is to say, in a Custom: For even a Custom is presum'd to be known unto all those Persons, that dwell in that Place, where such Custom has been introduc'd *. And a Prince is presum'd to be acquainted with all the vulgar and common Customs of the Place or Country that he governs. Again, this Presumption ought even to proceed, and take Place in all Edicts or Proclamations of Magistrates. For after a publick Promulgation thereof, an Edict or Proclamation is presum'd to be known unto all Persons therein or thereby concern'd. But some say, That

* *Bald.* in l. 2. C. S. 53.

It is not sufficient, that Laws are made by Legislators, and promulgated, unless Citizens or Subjects do receive the same, and approve of them by Usage: For if they are not receiv'd, they neither oblige the present Citizens or Subjects by their Force and Obligation, nor those that shall live or come hereafter. But it often happens to be a Doubt, whether after the Making and Promulgation of a Law, it may be presum'd to be receiv'd and approv'd of by the Use of Men? Wherein I agree with *Socinus*; that we ought not to presume such a Law has been receiv'd by Usage: And the Reason is, because even Privileges, which are called private or particular Laws, are not thus presum'd to be receiv'd by Usage; because whether this or that has been receiv'd by Usage, is a Matter which is never presum'd. When a Law is correctory and penal at the same Time, then the Masculine

Gen-

Gender do's not comprehend and include the Feminine *. All Laws in a doubtful Caſe ought * D. 2. 1.
to be underſtood, according to the Nature of 7.
the Title of them, under which they are plac'd; and a Law, that puniſhes a Man, who commits an Offence, comprehends alſo the Perſon that adviſes or commands the ſame. A Law or Statute, that ſpeaks in the Plural Number, has alſo Place in reſpect of one ſingle Perſon; and conſequently in the ſingular Number †. † C. 1. 2.
When one and the ſame Law has various Sig- 13.
nifications, it ought not to be alledg'd and quoted for the Deciſion of Cauſes; and the ſame thing may be ſaid of a Statute or Canon of the Church. When general Laws are made, they are underſtood to take away the particular Cuſtoms of Places and Statutes, if the Prince or Legiſlator be made acquainted with ſuch Laws ||. Altho' a penal Law ſpeaks perſonally, || C. 6. 23.
yet it comprehends the Perſon that commands 31.
ſuch an Offence to be committed. If one Law be corrected, other Laws, that tend to an Interpretation and Declaration of that Law, are underſtood to be corrected alſo by that Law. But every Law that deprives a Perſon of a Thing is not ſaid to be a penal Law; but only ſuch as is made *propter delictam.* The Canon and Feudal Law do both of them depend on the Knowledge of the *Roman* Law, and have a Coalition with it, as Members belonging to the ſame Body. Where a penal Law or Conſtitution ſpeaks by Words of the preſent or future Tenſe, as *cadat*, *privetur*, *amittat*, &c. There ſuch a Law ought to be underſtood, to mean by a Declaratory Sentence: And this is true, unleſs ſome *privative* Word be added

thereunto, as *statim*, *mox*, *eo ipso* or *omnino*, and the like; for then it is understood to mean *ipso Jure*. And 'tis the same Thing, *viz.* That a Declaratory Sentence is necessary, if the Law makes use of a Verb of the Præterperfect Tense, as *sit privatus*, &c. For when the Sense and Meaning of Words is doubtful, the Interpretation thereof ought to be made in *benigniorem partem*; and the Premises are true, whether the Penalty be *afflictive* or only *exclusive* of an *Action*, that is to say, in Bar of an Action. Yet where the Punishment is *prohibitive* of a Jurisdiction, when the Law says, *Non reddatur Jus*, then it ought to be taken and understood to mean *ipso Jure*. If any Doubt arises, *super Facto*, in a Punishment pronounc'd by Law, a Declaratory Sentence is necessary.

A Preface to a Law or Statute not only restrains the Sense and Meaning of such Law or Statute, according to *Bartolus* *. But it also denotes, the Mind and Intention of the Lawgiver, and proves the final Cause of such a Disposition or Order †. In a State or Commonwealth, Sovereign Power ought not to be given to the Laws alone, for two Reasons. *First*, Because there are some Laws, which are sometimes evil and unjust, *viz.* in a vicious Form of Commonwealths; as in a Tyrannical and Oligarchical Government, to which such Laws are accommodated: And he that obeys such Laws may be said to be a good Citizen or Subject, but not a good Man. *Secondly*, Because sometimes there are some Laws, which in respect of the Words themselves seem to be either obscure and ambiguous, or else too hard and rigorous: And there-

* In *l.* 8. D. 2. 15. 6.

† In *l.* D. 28. 5.

therefore they ſtand in need of ſome Equity, and the benign Interpretation of prudent and good Men. Nor ought Sovereign Power in a State or Commonwealth, to be committed and given to Men alone; becauſe all Men are liable to Paſſions, with which ſeveral are ſo far tranſported and hurry'd away, that they either cannot underſtand Truth and Juſtice, or elſe if they do, they cannot follow and practiſe them: And therefore in giving Judgment and pronouncing Sentence, they are very often miſtaken, and deviate from Truth and Juſtice. If this Sovereignty in a State was to be allowed to Men, it muſt either be granted to one Man alone, or to ſome few, or to all together. When 'tis granted to one alone, he is then a Perſon that excels in Virtue and Goodneſs, or ought (at leaſt) ſo to do.

When one and the ſame Law has ſeveral Meanings and Significations, ſuch Law ought not to be quoted for the Deciſion of Cauſes: And the ſame may be ſaid and obſerv'd of any Statute, Decree or Canon. Though a Law ſpeaks in the Perſon of one particular Man; yet it often ſeems to ſpeak in the Perſon and Name of an aggregate Corporation; and this Perſon is only deem'd to be put, and made uſe of there *exempli gratiâ*. When the Law ſpeaks indiſtinctly, we ought not to diſtinguiſh, unleſs this Diſtinction be made by ſome other Law. Whenever a Law or Statute requires three Citations, *per modum formæ*, one Citation will not do for all of them.

A Law that puniſhes Male-feazances or Miſdemeanours, is deem'd a favourable Law; and ought therefore to be extended. *Firſt*, It is to be obſerv'd, that in reſpect of Laws, one

Law may be determin'd and explain'd by another, whether these Laws are prior or posterior in point of Time to each other; so that one Law may be safely supply'd by another: But this ought to be understood with some Grains of Allowance, since new Laws do draw old Laws after them, either by supplying, determining or correcting them. But on the contrary, an old Law do's not draw a new Law after it, unless it be in the Point of determining such a Law. *Secondly*, 'Tis to be observ'd, that in Cases not express'd by Law may argue from Things of the like, to Things of the like Nature; since 'tis not possible in the Law to comprehend all Cases by Name. *Thirdly*, If there be a Doubt touching a Law, the Interpretation of that Law ought to be made by the Judge, or some Lawyer, either according to the Custom of the Place, if there be a Custom; but if there be no Custom, then it ought to be expounded in the more benign and better Sense; or if Necessity shall require it, Recourse ought to be had to the Prince or Sovereign Power. *Fourthly*, 'Tis to be observ'd, that no Answer ought to be given to a Law, unless the whole Law has been consider'd, for Precipitation is the Step-mother of Injustice. In all correctory Laws, Extension founded upon an Identity of Reason is ever lawful, when a Reason is expressed in a Law, that induces such a Correction: And it is the same Thing in Laws of Limitation, wherein an Extension founded upon an Identity of Reason is always lawful. But in correctory Laws an Extension is not lawful, which is founded even on a Majority of Reason. Extension in Correctories, is, when

re-

reduc'd to its firſt State and Primitive Right; and an Extenſion ought not to be made in Exorbitants.

Laſtly, There remains one Conſideration or Queſtion here to be diſcuſs'd, which is variouſly handled and diſputed by the Lawyers, touching that Power of making Laws, which the *Roman* People conferr'd on their Emperors; and it is this, *viz.* Whether and after what manner the Prince or Emperor may be ſaid to be exempt from the Laws, according to this Maxim of theirs, *viz. Princeps legibus ſalutus eſt.* Some of the Lawyers have thought this ſo wicked a Maxim, that it has brought ſeveral Calamities on the *Roman* State. But the Law of *Theodoſius* and *Valentinian* carries much more Humanity along with it, whereby they declare themſelves ſubject to the Laws: Thinking it fit and juſt, that a Prince ſhou'd conform himſelf, and ſhew Obedience to the Laws of the State. For nothing ought to be lawful for a Prince to do, which he forbids to his Subjects, ſince he ought not to condemn thoſe Laws in reſpect of himſelf, which he has Comenacted for the Uſe and Service of the Commonwealth. But ſome will underſtand *Ulpian* here to treat of Penal Laws, to which (they ſay) a Prince is not oblig'd: As the *Julian* and *Papian* Laws *De Pœnâ caduci* were, touching which Laws *Ulpian* there diſcourſes. But others do underſtand him, as ſpeaking of the Solemnities of the Civil Law in reſpect of Contracts, Judicial Proceedings, Laſt Wills and Teſtaments, and the like; to which Solemnities a Prince is not bound according to them, ſince his Preſence herein ſupplies all Solemnities of Law. But (I think) this Exemption do's not hold in respect of Contracts, Judicial Proceedings, Last Wills, *&c.* It is the Opinion of most Persons, that a Prince is bound both by the Law of Nature and Nations: And therefore since all these are founded on the Law of Nations, a Prince is surely bound by them. Thus according to *Baldus* and others, a Prince is bound by the Law of Nature or natural Reason, becausé the Law of Nature carries along with it greater Power than the Sovereignty. Wherefore it is said, That a Prince is bound by his Contract in the same manner as a private Man, and cannot rescind the same by any Plenitude of Power imaginable, since in every Contract what we call *Bona fides* is necessary. And hence it is, that Princes and Emperors are not exempt from the Law of Nature and of Nations. *Dion Cassius* says, That a Prince is obliged by such Laws as he stiles Laws of Necessity: And *Claud. Salmasius* observes, That when we say; That a Prince is bound by the Laws, it ought to be understood of such Contracts, as are introduc'd by the Law of Nations: As Bargain and Sale, Borrowing and Lending, Hiring and Letting to Hire, and such other commutative Contracts; for all Princes are oblig'd unto the Performance of these Contracts, and cannot in any wise by Prerogative exempt themselves from thence. Indeed it must be own'd with Grief and Sadness; that Despotick and Tyrannical Princes have asserted this Exemption from the Laws unto themselves, being supported in this extravagant Claim of Power not only by the Cruelty of the Sword, but also by the servile Flattery of of ſome Divines and Lawyers concurring with them herein, and making uſe of this knaviſh Diſtinction to ground their Opinion on, *viz.* That a Prince is bound to obſerve the Civil Laws of his Kingdom, only *vi directivâ*, that is to ſay, as theſe Laws are a Direction to him in the Adminiſtration of his Government, but not oblig'd (as they ſay) *vi coactivâ* by a compulſive Force; ſince no one can compel the Prince to the Obſervance of the Civil Laws. And this Opinion theſe State Sycophants wou'd found on the Law of Nature and Equity it ſelf: And, therefore, they think, that *Ulpian* only here ſpeaks of a *Coactive* or *Compulſive* Force.

Having treated of Laws in general, I ſhall now ſpeak of them in particular: And firſt of ſuch, as we ſtile Conſtitutions. For you muſt know, that ſuch Laws were ſtiled Conſtitutions, as were decreed by ſome *Roman* Emperor or other, that had a Deſign of making theſe Decrees into a Law*. In this Title, I ſhall conſider four Things. *Firſt*, How manifold the Conſtitutions of Princes are. *Secondly*, What Operation they have. *Thirdly*, After what manner Exemptions and Privileges are granted by Princes and Emperors. And, *Laſtly*, I ſhall have a regard to ſome Matters worthy Obſervation.

* D. i. 3. i.

As to the firſt, I find the Conſtitutions of Princes to be threefold, *viz.* a Conſtitution properly ſo called; a Privilege and a Reſcript. A Conſtitution is ſometimes made in a Judicial Manner, when the *Roman* Emperor pronounces Sentence †: And ſometimes extra-judicially, when any Thing is determin'd by way of Edict or Example, either with or without the Council of the Nobility, which yet

† C. i. 14. 12. i.

yet are comprehended in a Law. A Privilege is the Right of a private Person or Thing: If it respects a Person, it is called a Personal Privilege; but if it respects a Thing, then it is term'd a real Privilege. You have an Instance of a personal Privilege in the Tenth Book of the Code *; and of real Privileges you have many Examples in the Privileges of Cities and Corporations. Rescripts relate to Judicial Matters and the Administration of Justice †; and then they have not the Force of Law, unless it be in that Case, wherein a Rescript lies: Yet Rescripts are in a general Sense taken for all princely and royal Indults whatever ||. As to the second Point, *viz.* what Operation the Laws and Constitutions of Princes have, 'tis said, they have the Force of a written Law, but this in a various Manner: For if a Constitution be included in the Body of the Law, it always has the Force of a general Law: And 'tis the same Thing, if any Thing be decreed on the Cognizance of a Cause in the Presence of the Parties. But if it be not included in the Body of the Law, then it ought to be emitted by an interlocutory Sentence: Or if the Prince shall give a definitive Sentence without citing the Party, or without Cognizance of the Cause, tho' it be with his Nobles, otherwise called his *Palatines*, it makes indeed a Law, but not a general Law. For such a Constitution shall only have Operation between those Persons, among whom it was made. And 'tis the same Thing, if it be made on the Cognizance of a Cause, if it be made in Opposition to a written Law. For a Prince is not presum'd to be willing to destroy the Laws, but to confirm them, accord-

* *Tit.* 31. l. 61.

† X. 1. 3.

|| C. 1. 19.

according to *Salycetus* on the ſecond and third Law of this Title, and alſo on the twelfth Law quoted in the Margin *. Nor ought we to diſpute the Power of him that makes a Conſtitution, *viz.* Whether the Prince can make a Conſtitution or not; for he that diſputes this Power, incurs the Crime of Sacrilege †. Yet a Perſon may diſpute about the Will and Intention of the Prince, *viz.* Whether the Prince did it willingly, it being (perhaps) forced on him ||: For a Prince is preſum'd willing to do that which is juſt and equitable *, and conformable to the Laws †. But if a Prince decrees and ordains any Thing, *ex certâ Scientia & proprio Motu*, and from a Plenitude of Power, all Surreption and Obreption is deſtroyed and taken away ||; tho' the Doctors differ herein. Thus the Clauſe of *certa Scientia* has no Operation, unleſs it be in ſuch Things, as relate to ſome written Law or Fact, which the Prince may have ſome Knowledge of, eſpecially, if Clauſes do enſue, that are derogatory to a written Law *. But if the Iniquity be ſupervolitant and intolerable, the aforeſaid Clauſes according to *Baldus* in his *Conſil.* ſhall have no Operation at all; where he ſays, That the ſaid Clauſe which was raſhly apply'd by unskilful Counſellors, without making any Diſtinction of Things, ought to be eradicated the Court. But a Prince's Conſtitution has Operation in relation to the Law of God, when it diſtinguiſhes, but not when it takes away any Thing from thence. For tho' the Scripture ſays, *That in the Mouth of two or three Witneſſes, every Word ſhall be eſtabliſhed*; yet according to the *Civil* Law, a greater Number of Wit-

* C. 1. 14. 2 & 3. & 12.

† C. 1. 14. 12. c. 9. 29. 2.

|| *Bald.* in *l.* 2. c. 4. 29.

* D. 28. 6. 43.

† C. 7. 37. 2.

|| *Gloſs.* in *l.* 2. c. 7. 37.

* *Bald.* in *l.* fin. c. 7. 50.

Witnesses are necessarily required in Testaments, and other Matters.

Again, A Prince can decree nothing contrary to the Law of Nature and of Nations, especially, where the Act is touching the taking away of Things founded hereon; because he cannot deprive me of that which is mine by the Law of Nations, that is to say, by Contracts, *&c.* and give it to another *; unless it be on the score of some Crime committed, as in Persons condemn'd, and the like. But the Commands of a Prince shall have Operation against such Things as are ours by the Civil Law, if there be any derogatory Clauses. Yea, they shall operate against such Grants, as I shall obtain from the Prince by *mere Grace* and Privilege; or if the Thing be mine by the *Civil* Law as by Prescription, it may be taken from me by the Prince or Sovereign Power for the good of the State †. All these Matters are largely handled by *Felinus*, and others. As to the third Point, *viz.* after what manner Exemptions, Grants and Privileges of Princes ought to be understood; it is to be observ'd, That such as only respect the Right of the Person granting them, ought to be construed and taken in a very large Sense: But if they respect and concern the Interest of another, or be made against some written Law, they ought then to be expounded strictly. For doubtless, a Prince is presum'd so to provide for you, as not to injure me. The Sovereign Power of a Prince is chiefly discern'd in the Business of making and repealing Laws; the Power of making and repealing Laws, being granted only to the Prince or Emperor. But the Power of the *Roman* Emperor was heretofore

* Q. 1. 2 11.

† *Bald.* in *l.* 3. 6. 14.

fore not ſo great, as that his *Placarts* ſhou'd deſerve the Name and Stile of Laws: For the *Romans*, even after the Commonwealth was oppreſs'd by *Julius Cæſar*, retain'd the Legiſlative Power among themſelves; and has ſeveral other Badges and Traces of their popular Government and Democracy. For *Auguſtus* often asked the Conſent of the People, and intreated them to paſs ſuch an Act into a Law by way of Ordinance, which cou'd not be a Law without the Approbation of the People. But when the *Lex Regia* prevail'd, this Power of the People was almoſt extinguiſh'd and diminiſh'd; the People by that Law transferring all their Right and Power on one Perſon, whom they ſtiled Prince or Emperor.

What this *Lex Regia* was, and when it was made, is very uncertain; but 'tis moſt probable, that it was made under the Reign of *Octavianus Auguſtus*. For when the People firſt ſtiled him Prince of the Senate, he ſeem'd to refer all Things to the Intereſt and Advantage of the Publick. But it was afterwards the Pleaſure of the State, that he alone ſhould have the Care and Adminiſtration of the Commonwealth, under the Title of *Imperator* and *Auguſtus*; the Name of a King being odious to the *Romans*, thro' the Pride of the Kings depos'd. Hence it appears, that the People were depriv'd of their Power and Authority, which was always to remain in the Hands of this Prince or Emperor; and his Pleaſure being eſtabliſh'd as a Law, without ever conſulting the People, was to have the Name, Force, and Effect thereof. But as there is nothing ſo difficult as the making a Law, the Prince ought to make Uſe of the Senate as his Council in all Matters of Legislature. Nor ought a Prince to make too much Haste and Precipitation in the Making of Laws, lest his Laws should at some Time or other be displeasing even to himself. But he ought rather to follow the Custom and Practice of reading them over seven Times in the Consistory of his Palace, according to the Form used by the Emperors *Theodosius* and *Valentinian* before the Promulgation of any Law.

And in making of Laws 'tis necessary, That they should be general, just, honest, possible, profitable and manifest. General Laws belong to all Persons of the State in common: But particular Laws relate only to one certain Cause or Person, beyond which they do not extend, unless the Will of the Prince evidently declares it otherwise. For that which the Prince, or the Law, has determin'd in favour of any one, ought not to be wrested to his Disadvantage: Yet all Laws are unjust, unless they have a regard to the Good of the Publick. *Secondly*, Those Laws are therefore said to be just, that observe an Equality in giving to every one his due Right. And those are said to be honest, which contain nothing of Turpitude in them, or any Thing contrary to Decency and good Manners. *Thirdly*, Laws ought to be possible, since no one is oblig'd to Impossibilities; and it will be uncivil, and contrary to Humanity, to command a Man to do what he cannot do. Hence *Justinian* says, that in respect of Human Frailty, *Mediocres leges nostras ponimus*, We lay down such Laws as are practicable and easy to be complied with. *Fourthly*, Those Laws are said to be *profitable* which are not written for the Advantage of a private Person, or for the sake of Osten-

Oſtentation and Vain-glory; but for the common Benefit of all the Subjects of the State and Commonwealth. *Laſtly*, Laws ought to be clear and manifeſt, ſince nothing is ſo much the Property of Laws, as Simplicity, Clearneſs and Perſpicuity. For this Reaſon *Seneca* adviſes us, That Laws ought to be brief and ſhort, that the Unskilful may the better underſtand them; and that they may not be liable to Cavils and Wrangling. Wherefore he alſo adds, That nothing ſeems more frigid and fooliſh, than a Law with a Preface or Proem to it. And *Plato* ſays*, That tho' we ſee ſeveral Laws made with a Proem to them, ſhewing the Motive thereof, and with many Reaſons added thereunto, eſpecially in the *Novels* of *Juſtinian*; yet 'tis better to have fewer Laws thus publiſh'd than many; it being much more uſeful for a Perſon to expreſs himſelf in fit and proper Terms, than to tire out Men with ſeveral uſeleſs Words. And it cannot be otherwiſe, when there are many Laws, but that they muſt engender and multiply Law-Suits.

* *Lib.* 4. de Leg.

The final Cauſe of Laws, is, that Men may be ſafe and ſecure from Injuries by the Aid and Defence of Laws; that Vices may be corrected, and virtuous Men rewarded, which *Solon* ſtiles the Sheet-Anchor of any State or Commonwealth: And that Men in Power, with thoſe of the loweſt Rank, may hold ſuch Things in Poſſeſſion as they have legally purchas'd; and that they may be allow'd to alienate, and make all manner of lawful Contracts, which is the chief Foundation of civil Concord and Agreement. Hence *Cicero* ſays, That every good Law obſerves an Equality, confers a Security of Life, bridles

bridles the Desires of the Mind, by ordering Things just and honest; and forbids Things which are unjust and unseemly, by proposing Rewards for the Virtuous, and Punishments for vicious and wicked Doers. Therefore, since 'tis the Business of Laws to coerce and restrain the Lives of Men, by prescribing to them what they ought to pursue, and what they ought to avoid; it follows, that Laws ought to be conceiv'd and drawn with a Regard had to Futurity. And therefore they are said to give a Form to future Matters or Things hereafter, and not to have a Retrospect to Things or Matters past, although an ambiguous Term or Word shou'd be used therein; as, *Si quis fecerit*, and the like. By future Matters I do not here mean future Suits touching any Matter; but a future Matter, from whence a Suit may arise; as a Contract, last Will, a Trespass, and the like: For the Time of the Contract made, and not the Time of the Suit commenc'd, ought to be consider'd; unless (perhaps) there be a Law made which appertains to the Form and Order of judicial Proceedings, when such a Matter cannot be captious to any one. Yet sometimes Laws do extend their Authority to the Time past, as when they introduce no Thing new, but are only declaratory of some antient Law; or do confirm the same, or take away the Abuse of such a Law; or if the Crime committed be of so wicked and nefarious a Nature, that it threatens Ruin and Destruction to the Commonwealth, unless the same be punish'd, *&c.* Moreover, sometimes the Words of a Law may be expresly referr'd to the Time past; and when this happens, we do interpret a Law to have a Reſpect to Things paſt, leſt that Right which a Man lawfully acquires ſhou'd be taken away from him. But in Matters already adjudg'd, or decided, no Man ought to be prejudic'd by a new Law, altho' the Caſe be appeal'd *. But though a Law preſcribes unto Men a certain Rule of Life for the future, yet ſuch a Law is not a Cure and Remedy unto all Vices and Inconveniences, but is only adapted to ſuch as happen very often, and not to ſuch as happen but ſeldom: For all Caſes, which are ſometimes incident, cannot be particularly comprehended in the Laws.

* *Nov.* 115. cap. 1.

The general Effect of a Conſtitution is to oblige all Perſons ſubject thereunto, to the Knowledge and Obſervance thereof: Therefore, not only Lawyers, but even all other Perſons, are oblig'd to know and obſerve the Laws: Which I wou'd have to be underſtood touching ſuch Laws as are confirm'd by the Divine Command, or by the Sanction of natural Reaſon, made for the Inſtruction, and for Reſtraining the looſe Behaviour of inſolent Men; that hereby, the Preſcript of the Laws being evidently known unto all Men, they may either avoid ſuch Things as are forbidden them, or elſe follow ſuch Things as are permitted and allow'd them. But in other Reſpects (I think) no one is bound to know the Laws, beſides a Lawyer. But to know the Laws is not to bear the Words of them *memoriter* in a Man's Mind alone, but to underſtand the Force and Power of them. And tho' a Perſon does not act contrary to a Law, unleſs he does that thing which the Law expreſly forbids; yet the Lawyer *Paulus* writes, That he who circumvents and eludes the Intention thereof by

Salvo's, and escaping the Words of the Law, does act in *fraudem legis*: As when a Man gives Credit unto a Person under the Power of a Father, not by lending him Money, but something else, with a design of eluding the *Senatus Consultum Macedonianum*. Upon which Account the Emperor has *ipso jure* render'd null and void, not only whatever is done contrary to an express Prohibition of Law, but also, that which is done against the Mind and Intention of Law, altho' the Law has not expresly dictated or commanded the same: And such an Act is *ipso jure* null and void.

As to the Observance of Laws, it is certain, that all and every Person living within the Territory, unto which the Laws do extend themselves, are subject unto those Laws, and ought to yield them Obedience. From whence it comes to pass, That not only Subjects, and free Denizens, are bound thereby, but even Strangers also, so long as they continue, and have any fix'd Dwelling in another's Territory: But if they leave such Territory, they shall not be punish'd for any Crimes committed therein, during their Abode, by the Laws of such Territory, unless their own State, or the State unto which they fly, thinks fit to deliver them up to the Jurisdiction offended. Where a Law is not approv'd of by the Usage and Customs of the People that have the Use thereof, it does not render, and make the Transgressor of it to be an Offender. Nor is it convenient to right Reason, that one and the same Law should operate different Effects contrary unto each other. In penal Laws and Cases, Punishments ought rather to be restrain'd

and

and diminiſh'd, than amplify'd and increas'd. Where the Law is doubtful, and not very clear, the Judges ought to interpret it in ſuch a Manner as to be moſt conſonant to Equity, and leaſt inconvenient to the Subject: And that a Correction and Amendment of Laws may be avoided, a ſtrict Interpretation thereof ought to be made. A leſſer Evil ought to be tolerated in all Laws, that a greater Evil may be avoided.

Though the Prince, or Emperor, alone, can only make a general Law; yet particular Statutes may be made by other, and inferior Magiſtrates. *Bracton* ſays, That the Law makes the King: Therefore, let the King give unto the Law, that which the Law has given unto him, *viz. Dominion*; for he is not truly a King, whoſe Will governs and not the Law. The Reaſon of the Law is the ſame as the Law it ſelf: And therefore if the Reaſon of a Law ceaſes, the Order and Diſpoſition of ſuch Law likewiſe ceaſes with it. The Proſecution of the Law is indeed a grievous Vexation unto Men, but then the Execution of the Law finiſhes and crowns the Work; the Effect of the Law conſiſting in the due Execution thereof: For the Execution of the Law is ſaid to be the Fruit and End thereof; and this Execution cannot be ſaid to be injurious unto any one, if it be conformable to the Rules of Law.

PRIVILEGES.

THERE is this Difference between an *Indulgence* and a *Privilege, viz.* That an *Indulgence*, properly speaking, is a Dispensation which is not granted contrary to the common Law, but only contrary to some local Statutes or Laws: Whereas a *Privilege* is a proper and private Right, granted unto some Person or Body Politick contrary to the Rules of the common Law and common Right. And Privileges are an Abatement of common Right, because they are an Addition to the Right of a private Person, or Body Politick, so that a Privilege is either *personal* or *real.* A personal Privilege is that which is granted to any Person either contrary to, or besides the Course of the common Law. As for Example, That a Member of Parliament should not be arrested, nor any of his menial Servants, during the Sitting of Parliament. nor for any other limited Time before nor after. A personal Privilege follows the Person of him to whom it is granted; and it dies with him also, if the final Cause of granting such a Privilege be remov'd and extinguish'd: But where the final Cause of granting such a Privilege is not remov'd and extinguish'd by the Means or Death of the Person to whom it is granted; there (I say) such Privilege follows the Person of him to whom it is granted: For as the Effect ceases with the final

Cause

Cauſe thereof, ſo if the final Cauſe thereof does not ceaſe, the Effect continues and remains. A *real* Privilege is that which is granted to a Place, as to the two Univerſities of *Oxford* and *Cambridge*, *viz.* That no privileg'd Perſons thereof may be called to *Weſtminſter Hall* upon any Contract made within their own Precincts, or elſewhere, *infra Regnum Angliæ*; or upon the Account of any perſonal Plea whatſoever; or be proſecuted in any of the King's Courts. Nor can one belonging to the Court of *Chancery* be ſued in any other Court, unleſs it be in ſome certain Caſes excepted: For if he be thus ſued, he may remove the Suit by a Writ of Privilege grounded on the Statute of *Edward* the Third *. But the Quality of a Privilege, by the Change of the Perſons being in another Condition, is alſo chang'd; and conſequently the Privilege is loſt and extinguiſh'd thereby: As when a Man leaves the Court of *Chancery* and follows another Court; for perſonal Privileges ought not be extended to extraneous Perſons. Nor ought a Privilege granted to a Perſon to be extended to ſuch Things or Matters whereby the Advantage of the publick Weal may be injur'd and damnify'd. Altho' regularly every privileged Perſon may renounce and wave his Privilege, granted to him either by the Law or by the Prince, of impleading another, or of being impleaded himſelf in ſome certain Court belonging to ſuch Privilege, ſo that the Conſent or Leave of the ordinary Judge is not requir'd, the Parties Conſent being ſufficient: Yet in Caſes of mix'd Privileges it is otherwiſe. For altho' private Conſent makes him a Judge, that preſides over a Juriſdiction, yet the foregoing Rule

* 18 Ed. 3d *ch.*

proceeds no further than this, *viz.* That when the Privilege of such Court principally concerns Favour, and is granted for the Advantage of the Person waving his Privilege. Privileges ought always to be taken and understood in such a manner, as not to prejudice or diminish the Right of a third Person: Nor ought a Privilege to be a Refuge and Sanctuary for Delinquents, as in the *Romish* Church.

Cicero, in his Oration *pro domo suâ*, defines a Privilege to be a private Law, or Right conferred upon some particuar Person or Body Politick; and, according to another Author, it is a particular Law or Right, whereby a private Man, or a particular Corporation, is exempted from the Rigor of the common Law. It is sometimes used in our common Law for a Place that has a special Immunity granted to it. Privileges are Benefits and Matters of Grace, which are granted on the Account of Duty and good Offices; and, therefore, a contumacious and undutiful Subject may be rightly depriv'd of the Privileges granted to him on the Score of Duty and Obedience, because the Contumacy and Disobedience of Subjects towards their Leige Lords and Sovereigns, is an Offence of an heinous Nature, being cloathed with the utmost Ingratitude; and for such an Offence Privileges are lost and come to an end, since an Offence gives no Immunity to Delinquents. For the Authority of Crimes ought not to receive any Growth and Incouragement from a Pretence of Privileges granted, as in the Church of *Rome*, since they do hereby shake the Foundation of the publick Weal. But Privileges granted to an University, or Corporation, are not loſt by the Contravention of particular Perſons therein, unleſs they be encourag'd, or conniv'd at, by the ruling Power, in their Crimes and Exceſſes; for generally ſpeaking, the Offence of particular Perſons ought not to prejudice a Body Politick, or Corporation, without the aforeſaid Encouragement or Connivance given. The Loſs and Deprivation of Privileges, wherewith contumacious and diſobedient Subjects are uſually puniſh'd, ought, undoubtedly, to be reckon'd among the lighter Kinds of Puniſhments: For Privileges are ſuppos'd to be granted to Citizens and Subjects of a dutiful Temper and benevolent Diſpoſition, and to ſuch as will ſhew ſome ſort of Gratitude for them; and not to malevolent and rebellious Perſons. Therefore if the Motive, or final Cauſe, of granting ſuch Privileges does ceaſe, the Privileges themſelves ought to ceaſe. From hence it is, That Privileges granted to Scholars in Favour, and on the Account of their Studies, do not take Place, and extend themſelves to falſe, idle and loitering Students, altho' they be admitted into the Matriculation of the Univerſity, and the Catalogue or Regiſter of Scholars. Thus a Monk does not enjoy the Privileges of a true Monk, that is to ſay, the Privilege of his Order, from wearing his Habit only; becauſe the Habit does not make the Monk, but it is his Profeſſion, and a Diſcipline ſuitable to ſuch a Profeſſion.

A Privilege granted *durante Beneplacito*, which may be revoked at the Will and Pleaſure of the Granter, is at an end on the Death of the Perſon that granted the ſame: But a Privilege granted *Simpliciter*, and not at the Pleaſure

ſure of the Perſon that granted the ſame, is not extinguiſh'd and determin'd by his Death, but becomes perpetual: And the ſame Thing may be ſaid of a *Gratia* or *Beneplacitum.* Therefore, a Privilege granted *ad Beneplacitum*, laſts and continues, till ſuch Time as the Granter revokes the ſame, becauſe as a *Beneplacitum* is ſubject to no Law, it dies and expires with the Perſon himſelf, the Will of the Granter being diſſolv'd and extinguiſh'd by his Death. But by modern Uſage and Cuſtom it has obtain'd, that ſuch Privileges are not now revoked by the Death of the Granter; becauſe that which is not expreſly changed, is not prohibited to ſtand and remain. A Privilege granted contrary to the common Courſe of Privileges, is preſum'd to be falſe and ſurreptitiouſly obtain'd. The Inſinuation or Intimation of Privileges ought to be made in the Preſence of a competent Judge, or before a Notary, or two Witneſſes: And Privileges not intimated to the Party, are of no Advantage to a Man in his Cauſe.

A Privilege is not preſum'd, but it ought to be ſet forth and proved, ſince it is a matter of Fact: And he that alledges or ſets forth a Privilege, ought to prove the ſame in the beſt manner he may. But a Privilege is not prov'd *per uſum Privilegii*, but by a juſt and legal Title unto ſuch Privilege. For in Privileges properly ſpeaking there lies no Preſcription, becauſe he that avers a Privilege alledges *malam fidem*, unleſs he proves a good Title to ſuch Privilege. The Title of a Phyſician here in *England* do's not privilege a Perſon, that is choſen Conſtable of a Pariſh: For there is a Diffe-

Difference between an Attorney or Barriſter at Law, and a Phyſician: The former enjoy their Privilege by Reaſon of their Attendance in publick Courts; and not on the Account of private Buſineſs in their Chambers: But a Phyſician's Buſineſs is a private Calling only.

LIBRI JURIDICI.

FOLIO.

CORPUS juris civilis, 2 *Vol.* 1514
Corpus juris civilis cum gloſs. & caſ. *&c.* 6 *Vol.* *Lugd.* 1618
Corpus juris civilis cum gloſs. & caſ. *&c.* 6 *Vol.* *Aurel.* 1625
Corpus juris civilis cum Gothofredi not. 2 *Vol.* *Amſt.* 1663
Corpus juris civilis cum Gothofredi not. 2 *Vol.* *Lugd.* 1650
Corpus juris civilis cum Gothofredi not. 2 *Vol.* *ibid.* 1590
Corpus juris civilis, 2 *Vol.* ap. Car. *Plant.* 1575
Pandectarum 50 Libri ex Florentin Pandect. Repræſent. 2 *Vol.* 1553
Pandectæ juris civilis ex editione Herugiana *Baſ.* 1541
Idem ex editione Hugon. de Porta ad Florent. exem. *Lugd.* 1542
Idem ex editione Hug. de Porta ad idem exemplar *Lugd.* 1552.

Co-

Codex Juftinianæus, 5 *Vol.* *Par.* 1566

Codex Theodofianus cum Gothofred comm. 6 *Vol.* *Lugd.* 1665

Corpus juris canonici cum glofs. & caf. 3 *Vol.* 1671

Corpus juris canonici cum glofs. & caf. 3 *Vol.* *Paris* 1612

Ærodii pandect. jur. civil. per Phil. Oldenburg *Gen.* 1678

Abbatis Panormitani opera omnia, 5 *Vol.* *Lugd.* 1547

Auguftini antiquæ decretalium collectiones *Par.* 1621

Ejufdem juris pontificii veteris epitome *ibid.* 1641

Ejufdem antiquæ decretalium decifiones *Ilerd.* 1579

Anton. Auguftini epitome juris pontificii, 2 *Vol.* *Rom.*

Alterii tractatus de cenfuris ecclefiafticis, 2 *Vol.* *ibid.*

Alciati opera omnia juridica, 3 *Vol.* *Baf.* 1571

Alexandri opera omnia juridica, 6 *Vol.* *Lugd.* 1539

Johan. Andreæ comment. in decretales, 2 *Vol.* *Ven.* 1612

Francis de Acceptantibus de fentent. dittin. & Inter. *Ven.* 1584

Azrii quæftiones & refolutiones juris

Francis de Accoltis in primi, fecundi, *&c.* decretal. comment. *Ven.* 1581

Ejufdem comment. in fecundam partem digeft. *&c.* *ibid.* 1589

Non. Acoftæ tractatus de privilegiis creditorum *Rom.* 1661.

Accromboni repetitiones in jure civili Rom. *Lugd.* 1553

Petri

Petri Alegonæ compendium juris canonic. 2 *Tom.* *ibid.* 1623

Albanus de potestate Papæ & concilii *Ven.* 1584

Andreæ Alciati opera omnia juridica, 4 *Tom.*

Anton. Augustinus de propriis nominib. pandect. Flor. *Par.* 1579

Matth. de Afflictis de privilegiis fisci tractat. *Bas.* 1550

Authores varii de jurisdictione Imperiali *ibid.* 1559

Aymonis comment. in consuetudines Arverniæ

D'Arevedo in constitutiones regias Hispanicas

Baldi opera omnia juridica, 5 *Vol.* *Lugd.* 1585

Bartoli opera omnia juridica, 5 *Vol.* *Aug. Taur.* 1577

Ejusdem opera omnia juridica, 5 *Vol.* *Basil* 1562

Bartoli distinctiones juris *ibid.*

Baldi comment. in digest. & cod. 3 *Vol.* 1616

Bardi Margarita nova & singularis *Bon.* 1497

Balzarani comment. in constitutiones Siculas

August. Barbosa de potestate & officio episcoporum 1656

Ejusdem collectanea, D.D. in jus pontificium 1656

Ejusdem collectanea, D. D. in jus pontificium *Lugd.* 1637

Ejusdem tractatus de canonicis & dignitatibus *ibid.* 1658

Idem de jure ecclesiastico universo, 2 *Vol.* 1660

Ejusdem collectanea, D. D. in cod. Justin. 2 *Tom.* *Lugd.* 1660

Ejusdem tractatus de matrimonio *ibid.* 1668

Baronis opera omnia juridica ap. Morellum, 3 *Vol.* 1598

Guil. de Benedetto repetitiones juris *Lugd.* 1575

Bengerus & Pinsonius de beneficiis eccles. *Par.* 1654

Bellugæ speculum principum 1530

Belloni

Belloni tractatus de jure accrescendi
Barry tractatus de successionibus
Bibliotheca juris veteris canonici, 2 *Vol.* 1661
Bibliotheque du Droit Francois, 3 *Vol.* 1619
Bibliotheque des Arrests
Borelli comment. in statuta Parmensia
Bonacinæ opera omnia juridica, 2 *Vol. Lugd.* 1634
Bordoni opera omnia juridica, 5 *Vol.* 1665
Brachylogi. totius juris civil. summ. seu corpus legum *Lugd.* 1559
Bredorodii sententiarum jur. & regul. repertorium *Lugd.* 1607
Ejusdem tractatus de appellationibus
Brissonius de Formulis veterum Romanor.
Brunemanni comment. in pandect. & cod. *Fran.* & *Lipf.* 1716
Bochelli decreta ecclesiæ Gallicanæ *Par.* 1609
Borgalii tractatus de dolo *Han.* 1604
Bucherii Belgium Roman. eccles. & civilis *Leod.* 1655
Budæi commentaria in pandectas
Ejusdem Forensia
Barbosæ repertorium juris civil. & canonici *Lugd.* 1668
Claud. Coteræus de jure & privilegiis militum 1639
Cujacii opera omnia juridica, 10 *Vol. Paris* 1658
Corasii miscellanea juris
Choppinus de jure cœnobitarum *Paris* 1650
Idem de legibus Andium municipalibus *ibid.* 1581
Cœvallos de cognitione per viam violent. in caus. eccles. *Lot.* 1620
Covarruviæ opera omnia juridica, 2 *Vol.* 1661
Ejusdem opera omnia juridica, 2 *Tom. Lugd.* 1606
Charondas annotations on Hen. 3d, French code *Par.* 1615

Car-

Carpzovii definitiones ecclesiasticæ 1665
Ejusdem rerum criminalium praxis Saxonica *Witteb.* 1677
Cyni in veteris digesti libros comment. *Lugd.* 1547
Julii Clarii opera omnia juridica *Genev.* 1666
Ejusdem pract. civil. & criminalis *Lugd.* 1661
Innocent. Cyronii opera in jus canonicum *Thol.* 1645
Corpus juris Russardi notis, 2 *Vol.* *Lugd.* 1561
Cherubini magnum bullarium Roman. 6 *Vol.* *Rom.* 1638
Codex Fabrianus de definitionib. forensibus *Lugd.* 1649
Ejusdem definitiones forenses *Fran.* 1612
Carponi comment. in statuta Mediolensia
Hieron. Cœvallos aureum speculum ex recent. edit. *Col.* 1664
Donelli opera omnia juridica, 4 *Vol.* *Han.* 1611
Ejusdem opera omnia juridica, 4 *Vol.* *Franc.* 1590
Durandi speculum juris, cum addit. *ibid.* 1612
Ejusdem speculum juris cum additam. *ibid.* 1592
Ejusdem speculum juris cum additam. *Bas.* 1574
Ejusdem speculum juris cum additam. *Lugd.* 1551
Duarchi in jus civile opera omnia *Franc.* 1592
Formosinus de legibus ecclesiasticis 1662
Arnold. Ferroni comment. in consuetudin. Burdigalens. 1565
Fenronii jus municipale urbis Romæ *Rom.* 1665
Prosp. Farinacii opera omnia juridica, 13 *Vol.* 1622
Ejusdem tractatus de testibus *Fran.* 1598
Ejusdem opera criminalia, 4 *Vol.* *ibid.* 1602
Fontanella de pactis nuptialibus 1659
Fabri rationalia in pandectas juris, 5 *Vol.* 1659
Fabri syntagma triplex juris civilis & canonici *Gen.* 1689

Fer-

Ferretti prælectiones in jus civile *Lugd.* 1553
Fleta cum notis Seldeni *Lond.* 1647
Fagnani comment. in 5 libros decretalium, 2 *Vol.* *C. Ag.* 1681
Anton. Fabri conjecturæ juris civilis 1661
Felini Sandæi comment. ad 5 libros decretal. *Lugd.* 1590
Anton. Garronis comment. ad tit. de origin. juris 1543
Garciæ comment. in tit. de pactis *Ven.* 1587
Ejusdem variæ repetitiones in jure civili *Lugd.* 1533
Guazzini opera criminalia, 2 *Vol.* 1676
Gudelini commentar. de jure novissimo 1644
Bernard. Greven practicæ conclusiones 1644
Gomesii comment. variæque resolution. jur. civ. 3 *Tom.* *Antv.* 1634
Garratus seu Garatus Laudens. de crimin. læs. Majestat. *Fran.* 1587
Ejusdem tractatus de primogenitura
Ejusdem tractatus de repressaliis *Lugd.* 1593
Ejusdem tractatus de monetis *Col. Ag.* 1591
Ejusdem tractatus de bello *Ven.* 1584
Ejusdem tractatus de cardinalibus *ibid.* 1584
Ejusdem tractatus de legitimatione *ibid.* 1584
Ejusdem tractatus de privilegio *ibid.* 1584
Ejusdem tractatus de legatis principum
Ejusdem tractatus de Castellanis & Castris
Garionius de fœminis ad feuda recipiendis, *&c.* *Ven.* 1584
Antonii Gabrielis conclusiones *Fran.* 1576
Joh. Gruttererre practicæ conclusiones *ibid.* 1607
Goldasti collectio legum imperialium *ibid.* 1674
Garciæ tractatus de beneficiis *Genev.* 1658
Anton. Goveani opera juris civilis *Lugd.* 1564

Joh.

Joh. de Gradibus addit. ad Fabri lectur. in 4 lib. institut. 1543
Gozadini variæ repetitiones in jure civil. *Lugd.* 1553
Ejusdem repetitiones in l. *omnes populi* F. *Bon.* 1561
Goustæus de potestate regiâ in ecclesiam *Fran.* 1621
Hojeda de compatibilitate beneficiorum *Ven.*
Hotatii montani tractatus de regalibus 1634
Heiminsel dii statuta & præscripta imperialia, *&c.* 1607
Heraldi quæstiones quotidianæ & ejusdem observat. ad Salmasium de jure Attico & Romano *Par.* 1650
Herburti statuta regni Poloniæ *Dant.* 1620
Herveti constitutiones imperiales *Han.* 1606
Hotomanni opera omnia juridica, 3 *V. Lugd.* 1599
Hoppingius de insignium & armorum jure *Norim.* 1642
Joh. Heroldi liber Germanic. antiquit. & orig. *&c.* *Bas.* 1557
Hilligeri Donellus enucleatus *Antw.* 1642
Heringii tractatus de fide jussoribus 1675
H. Seg. Hostiensis aurea summa *Colon* 1612
Heroldi origines & leges antiquæ var. popul. *Bas.*
Imolensis comment. super Clementinas *Lugd.* 1539
Ejusdem comment. sup. primum, secundum, & tertium decretal, 3 *Vol.* *Lugd.* 1525
Jus regni Neapolitani *Neap.* 1605
Jus succedendi in Lusitaniæ regnum *Par.* 1641
Jus provinciale ducatûs Prussiæ 1620
Jasonis Magni comment. juris, 5 *Vol.* 1592
Justiniani institutiones Græcè ap. H. Steph. 1558

Lindenbrogi codex legum antiquarum, 2 *Vol*, *Fran.* 1613
Lucii placitorum ſummæ apud Gallos curiæ 1559
Rob. Lancellottus de attent. & innovatis *Franc.* 1652
Mantica de conjecturis ultim. voluntatum *ibid.* 1580
Marquardus de jure mercatorum 1662
Andreas de Mendo de jure academico *Lugd.* 1668
Mudæi tractatus de contractibus
Molinæi opera omnia juridica, 4 *Vol.* *Paris* 1612
Maſcardi tractatus de probationibus, 4 *Vol.* *Fran.* 1651
Molfeſii Praxis contractuum ult. voluntatum & de ſepultur *Neap.* 1622
Menochii opera omnia juridica, 4 *Vol.* *Genev.* 1687
Maſcardi tractatus de probationibus, 3 *Vol.* *Franc.* 1558
Marta de juriſdictione eccleſiaſticâ & ſæculari *Mog.* 1610
Mornacii opera omnia juridica, 3 *Vol.* *Par.* 1654
Menochii tractatus de præſumptionibus
Ejuſdem quæſtiones & præſumptiones juris
Murgæ tractatus de beneficiis eccleſiaſticis 1684
Matthæi à Coronâ poteſtas ſpiritualis epiſcoporum
Omphalii tractatus de uſurpatione legum *Baſ.* 1550
Oldendorpii tractatus de actionib. forenſibus *Colon* 1544
Alp. de Olea tractat. de ceſſione jurium & Actionum
Pancirolli Theſaurus utriuſque juris lection *Venet.* 1611
Ejuſdem notitia dignitatis utriuſque Imperii *Lugd.* 1608

Ejusdem notitia dignitatis utriusque Imperii *Ven.* 1593
Peckii opera omnia juridica 1666
Paciani tractatus de probationibus 1631
Pacii synopsis utriusque juris 1620
Perezii prælectiones in codicem Justinianæum 1656
Paponii corpus juris Gallici seu rhapsodiæ *Colon.* 1624
Pauli Angli aureum speculum de plenit. potest. Pap. *Fran.* 1621
Franc. de Pavinis de officio & potest. capit. sede vacant. *Ven.* 1584
Perusini in Sexti Decretalium comment. *Bas.* 1581
Frederic. Prackmanni opuscula politico-jurid. 3 *Vol.* *Fran.* 1672
Pergas resolutiones forenses *Ulyssip.* 1668.
Peregrini tractatus selecti practici *Ven.* 1611
Pithæi codex legum Visigothorum
Harman. Pistoris juris Roman. & Saxonic. quæst. 1604
Petiti leges Atticæ *Paris* 1635
Photii nomocanon *Basil* 1601
Sim. de Pratis de interpret. ultim. voluntatum *Col. Ag.* 1583
Quintinus de dispensationibus beneficiorum
Rævardi opera omnia juridica, 3 *Vol.* 1623
Rosenthal tractatus & synopsis jur. feudal. 2 *Tom.* 1616
Rebuffi tractatus de beneficiis *Lugd.* 1620
Rodriquez de concursu & privilegiis creditorum *Gen.* 1661
Rubæus de morientium eleemosynis
Ruffini collatio legum Mosaicarum
Schilteri praxis jur. Romani in foro Germanico *Fran.* 1713

Salas

Salas tractatus de legibus *Lugd.* 1611
Scotiæ veteres leges cum Skenæi notis *Edin.*1609
Joh. Scilteri comm. in jus civ. ſeu praxis juris Romani in foro Germanico, *&c.* *Jenæ.* 1698
Gonçales Suarez praxis eccleſiaſtic. & ſæcular. 3 *Tom.* *Metim.*
Salgado tractatus de regiâ protectione, 2 *V.*1667
Sarmiento de reditibus eccleſiaſticis tractatus
Sanchez tractatus de matrimonio *Lugd.* 1669
Ejuſdem tractatus de matrimonio *Antw.* 1607
Scacciæ tractatus de commerciis & cambiis, *Romæ* 1619
Suarez tractatus de legibus & legiſlatorib. *Lond.* 1679
Spelmanni concilia Anglicana, 2 *Vol.* *ibid.* 1639
Sigonius de jure antiquo Romanorum, *Han.*1609
Idem de jure antiquo Romanorum *Franc.*1592
Scacciæ tractatus de appellationibus 1628
Ejuſdem tractatus de ſententiâ & re judicatâ 1628
Solerzano de jure Indiarum tractat. 2 *Vol.* *Lugd.* 1672
Skenæi tractatus de regiâ poteſtate & majeſtate *Edinb.* 1609
Surdi tractatus de alimentis *Genev.* 1645
Tiraquellus de nobilitate & jure primogenitorum 1566
Ejuſdem tractatus de utroque retractu municipali, *&c.* *Lugd.* 1571
Ejuſdem tractatus de legibus connubialibus
Ejuſdem opera omnia juridica, 2 *Vol.* *Franc.*1616
Idem de locis legum temperandis & remittendis
Tractatus tractatuum in utroque jure, 28 *Vol.* *Ven.* 1584
Tholoſani ſyntagma juris univerſi *Genev.* 1623
Ejuſdem ſyntagma juris univerſi, 2 *Vol.* *Fran.* 1596, *Han.* 1612

Tartagni comment. in primum & ſecundum lib. 3. *Vol.* 1619

Theſaurus communium opinionum in jure *Fran.* 1616

Tuldeni comment. ad codicem Juſtinianæum *Lovan.* 1632

Theophili inſtitutiones juris Græcè ap. Froben *Baſ.* 1534

Thomaſii decades tractatuum *Patav.* 1642

Cardinalis Tuſchi opera jurid. 8 *Tom.* 4 *Vol.* *Lugd.* 1661

Ejuſdem opera omnia juridica, 8 *Vol. ibid.* 1634

Laurent. Vallæ tractatus de judice ſuſpecto

Vigelii methodus univerſi juris civilis

Valentis concordantia juris pontificii cum Cæſareo 1654

Vaſquius de ſucceſſionibus & ultim. voluntatibus *Franc.* 1610

Andreas Vallius de ſupremâ poteſtate Papæ *Paris* 1614

Voetii pars prior comment. ad pandectas *L. Batav.* 1698

Ejuſdem pars altera continens poſteriores *Hagæ.* 1704

Alvarez de Velaſco judex perfectus *Lugd.* 1620

Werbuzus de conſuetudinibus & decretis Hungariæ 1628

Windelini leges Salicæ cum Gloſſario *Antw.* 1649

Udalrici Zazii opera omnia juridica, 3 *Vol. Franc.* 1590

Zocſii commentaria in pandectas *Lovan.* 1667

Zazii (Udalrici) tractatus de actionibus *Baſil* 1537

Alexandri conſilia ſive reſponſa juris *Ven.* 1595

Alciati conſilia ſive reſponſa juris *Baſil* 1582

Jacob.

Jacob. Æmyliani consilia sive responsa juris *Ven.* 1565

Albani varia consilia sive responsa juris *Rom.* 1553

Franc. de Albergotis consilium matrimoniale *Franc.* 1580

Joh. de Anania consilia sive responsa juris *Lugd.* 1540

Baldi consilia sive responsa juris 2 *Vol.* 1686

Jusdem consilia sive responsa juris 2 *Vol. Ven.* 1608

Antonii de Butrio consilia sive responsa juris *Ibid.* 1582

Scholia ad Consilia Antonii de Butrio *Ibid.* 1582

Petri de Ancherano consilia sive responsa juris *Ibid.* 1585

Petri Belli consilia sive responsa juris

Bardeloni consilia sive responsa juris

Barbatiæ consilia sive responsa juris 2 *Vol.*

Ægid. Bellameræ consilia sive responsa juris

Calderini consilia sive responsa juris *Ven.* 1582

Pauli de Castro consilia sive responsa juris *Amber.* 1607

Cacherani consilia sive responsa juris *Franc.* 1599

Laurent. Calcanei consilia sive responsa juris *Lugd.* 1549

Castilionis consilia sive responsa juris

Joh. Bapt. Cæsaris consilia sive responsa juris *Franc.* 1678

Cornei consilia sive responsa juris 2 *Vol.*

Caballi consilia decisiva in causis civilibus *Ven.* 1607

Aymonis Cravettæ consilia sive responsa juris 2 *Vol.* 1611

Decii consilia sive responsa juris *Ibid.* 1581

Evartii consilia sive responsa juris 1603

Fichardi consilia sive responsa juris *Franc.* 1590
Giurbæ consilia sive responsa juris *Col. Agr.* 1629
Grillinzonii consilia sive responsa juris 1614
Hotomanni consilia sive responsa juris 1586
Jasonis Magni consilia sive responsa juris *Ven.* 1581
Joh. de Imola consilia sive responsa juris *Franc.* 1580
Kinscoti consilia sive responsa juris 1653
Leonini centuria consisiorum juris *Antw.* 1584
Leonissæ consilia matrimonialia *Franc.* 1580
Mynsingeri consilia sive responsa juris *Basil.* 1573
Menochii consilia sive responsa juris 1628
Philippi Monspeliensis consilia sive responsa juris *Lugd.* 1584
Antonii Nattæ consilia sive responsa juris 3 *Tom.* *Ven.* 1584
Oldradi consilia sive responsa juris *Lugd.* 1550
Guidonis Papæ consilia sive responsa juris *Franc.* 1594
Johannis Fran. de Ponte consilia sive responsa juris 2 *Vol.* *Gen.* 1666
Modestini Pistoris consilia sive responsa juris 2 *Vol.* *Lip.* 1596
Simonis Pistoris consilia sive responsa juris 2 *Vol.* *Lips.* 1596
Rebuffi consilia sive responsa juris *Lugd.* 1618
Salerni consilia sive responsa juris
Roderici allegationes & consilia juris *Vallis,* 1588
Smidii consilia Argentorensia 2 *Vol.* *Argent.* 1601
Petri Surdi consilia sive responsa juris 1629
Tartagni consilia sive responsa juris 2 *Vol.* 1618
Wesembecii consilia sive responsa juris *Franc.* 1600
Zabarellæ consilia sive responsa juris *Ven.* 1581
Ziletti consilia matrimonialia 2 *Vol.* *Franc.* 1580
Ejusdem consilia criminalia *Ibid.* 1576

Wern-

Wernkeri Themarensis consilium juris *Ibid.* 1589
Lauderchii consilia sive responsa juris *Ferrar.* 1600
Mariani Socini consilia sive responsa juris *Ven.* 1580
Paul. Æmylii decisiones causarum sacri palatii Apostolic *Ven.* 1585
Augustini summa Apostolicarum decisionum
Barbosæ summa Apostolicarum decisionum 1658
Bellonii decisiones rotæ Genuæ de mercatura *Ven.* 1582
Corvini decisiones rotæ Romanæ 1647
Caballi resolutionum criminalium centuriæ *Flor.* 1606
Georg. de Cabedo practicæ decisiones senat. Lusitan. *Antw.* 1620
Boerii decisiones aureæ juris *Lugd.* 1544
Durandi decisiones rotæ Romanæ *Ibid.* 1638
Maynardi decisiones novæ Tholosanæ Latine *Franc.* 1610
Ludov. à Pegueræ decisiones civiles & criminal. *Aug. Taur.* 1613
Guidonis Papæ decisiones cum ann. *Col. Agr.* 1643
Jacobi Putei decisiones juris *Colon.* 1582
De Vargas Machutæ decisiones regni Arragoniæ *Neap.* 1676
Decisiones feudales variorum cum aliis decisionibus senatus Pisani *Spir.* 1605
Anton. Barræ controversiæ forens. cum decisionibus *Neap.* 1680
Calvini lexicon juridicum *Genev.* 1670
Macri dictionarium ecclesiasticum
Alberici de Rosate dictionarium juridicum *Ven.* 1601
Scardii lexicon juridicum *Colon. Ag.* 1593
Ejusdem lexicon juridicum *Colon.* 1600

Barnabæ Briſſonii lexicon juridicum *Franc.* 1587
Spigelii lexicon juridicum *Baſil.* 1577
Cujacii conſtitutiones imperiales 8 libris *Han.* 1606
Baluzii capitula & conſtitutiones Francorum 2 *Vol.* *Paris* 1677
Epiſtolarum decretalium pontificiar. collect. 3 *Vol.* 1591
Baſilikῶν libri 60 Gl. per Fabrollum 7 *Vol.* *Paris* 1647
Antonius Frances de eccleſiis cathedralibus
Fran. de Imaya opera juridica
Haloandri analyſis inſtitutionum imperial. 1574
Anton. Fabri rationalia ad pandectas *Tom.* prim. *Gen.* 1604
Ejuſdem rationalia ad pandectas *Tom.* ſecundus *Ibid.* 1619
Ejuſdem rationalia ad pandectas *Tom.* tertius *Colon.* 1624
Ejuſdem codex Subaudicus ad ordin. cod. Juſtin. *Franc.* 1612
Ejuſdem codex Subaudicus ad ordinem cod. juſt. *Lugd.* 1649
Lavorii varia de jure canonico *Romæ*
Martæ Neapolitani digeſta noviſſima 1622
Ejuſdem tractatus de ſucceſſione legati 1624
Maſii ſingularium opinionum lib. in jure civ. *Lov.* 1630
Volutii Metiani tractatus de aſſe *Paris* 1586
Darii Meuii comment: in jus Lubecenſe
Modii praxis rerum criminialium *Franc.* 1587
Anton. Nattæ repetitiones in jure civili *Lugd.* 1553
Montirenſius in ſtatua Bononienſia 1582
Garavitæ comment. in ſtatuta Neapolitana 1601
Steph. Vinand Pighii annales magiſtratuum & provinciarum ſenatus populiq; Romani ab urb. *Condita*, *Antw.* 1599

Or-

Ordenancas de la Real audiencas 7 chancellaria *Gran.* 1601

Statuta Subaudiæ.

Sota in constitutiones Subaudiæ

Anton. de Sousa decisiones suprem. senat. Lusitan. *Ulyss.* 1676

Jacob Alvarotti tractatus de feudis *Fran.* 1587

Paul. Fuschus de visitatione & regimin. ecclesiar. *Rom.* 1581

Rudorfi vindiciæ causæ Palatinæ 1640

Caroli Sigonii de judiciis libri tres *Paris* 1576

Ejusdem tractatus de judiciis *Han.* 1609

Novellæ constitutiones cura Hervagii & Scrimger. *Basil* 1541

Novellæ constitutiones ex bibliotheca Fuggeri *Ibid.* 1558

Haloandri versio Novellarum per Lud. Russard. edit. *Paris* 1557

Straccæ tractatus de mercatura

Gabrielis consilia sive responsa juris 2 *Vol. Ven.* 1596

Corpus juris canonici *Paris* 1618

Magnum Bullarium Romanum cherubini 5 *Vol. Lugd.* 1673

Daoyz index juris civilis *Aurel.* 1625

Daoyz index juris pontificii 2 *Vol. Burd.* 1623

Gomesii comment in leges Taurinas *Antw.* 1617

Bartolus a Saxeferrato cum Alex. Barb. Par. *&c.* Annot. 5 *Vol.*, *Lugd.* 1581

Gudelini syntagma regular. utriusque juris *Antw.* 1646

Corpus juris canonici 3 *Vol.* *Lugd.* 1584

Hautin patrocinium defunctorum *Leod.* 1664

Mastrilli tractat. de magistratib. & eorum imperio *Lugd.* 1621

Castellianus Cotta de jurisperitis *Ven.* 1584

Joh.

Joh. Filesacus de parœciarum & parœcorum origine

Franc. Broei expositiones ad 4 libros institution. *Paris* 1622

Ejusdem chronologica historia totius juris *Ibid.*

Nic. Eymerici directorium inquisitorum hæres *Ven.* 1607

Frid. Schenk. interpretatio in 3 libr. usuum feud. *Col.* 1555

Hen. de Bowick tractatus de jure patronatus *Franc.* 1581

Ejusdem distinctiones super 5 libros Decretalium *Lugd.* 1498

Marc. Mant. Bonavidii tract. de jure protimysios. *Franc.* 1588

Berrandi consiliorum juris 8 *Vol.* *Franc.* 1603

Besoldi conclusiones de jure universitatum *Tub.* 1621

Idem de Comitibus & Baronib. imperii German. *Ibid.* 1619

Mornacii observat. ad 24 lib. ff. & 4 lib. cod. *Par.* 1631

Ejusdem syntagma juris civilis

Compendium Schutzianum juris civilis

Joh. Voetii ad pandectas prior pars *L. Batav.* 1698

Ejusdem ad pandectas pars altera *Hag. Com.* 1704

Joh. Hen. Bergeri comment. ad codicem *Franc.* & *Lips.* 1716

Hon. Hahnii observationes ad Wesembecium *Helmst.* 1668

Ejusdem observationes ad Wesembecium *Helm.* 1706

QUARTO.

Corpus juris civilis, 2 *Vol.* 1514
Corpus juris civilis, cum Gloſs. & Caſib. 6 *Vol.* ap. Junt. *Ven.* 1621
Corpus juris civilis cum Gloſs. & Caſ. 5 *Vol.* *Paris* 1550
Corpus juris civilis, cum Gloſs. *Lugd.* 1583
Les loix civiles par Domat 6 *Vol.* *Paris* 1697
Corpus juris canonici cum Gloſs. & not. Molinæi *Lugd.* 1559
Corpus juris canonici cum Gloſs. *Colon* 1631
Aurelius de rebus judicial. *Paris* 1611
Anton. Auguſtinus de legibus & ſenatus-conſult. Roman. Urſin. not. *Par.* 1585
Ejuſdem tractatus de legibus & ſenatus-conſult. Roman. *Rom.* 1583
D'Avila tractatus de cenſuris eccleſiaſticis *Lugd.* 1608
Abregè de la juris-prudence Romaine 1671
Albenſis tractatus de re militari & bello 1562
Alzedo de functionibus epiſcoporum tractatus *Ludg.* 1630
Acta ſynodi Florentinæ Græcè & Latinè *Flor.*
Acta concilii Conſtantinopolitan. 4ti Gl. per Raderum 1604
Acta concilii primi Piſani & concilii Senenſis 1612
Alteſerræ tractatus de fictionibus juris *Paris* 1659
Ejuſdem diſſertationes de jure canonico
Abbatis Panormitani opera, 8 *Tom.* 5 *Vol.* *Ven.* 1588
Arumæi tractatus de jure publico, ap Junt. 1613

Actii tractatus de ludo Schaccarum 1585
Abregè de la juris-prudence Romane per Colomber 1653
Allæ tractatus de advocato & causidico Christiano *Crem.* 1610
Alexandri tractatus de regionibus suburbicariis *Paris* 1619
Franc. de Amayæ observationes juris *Genev.* 1633
Arnizæus de authoritate principum in populum 1612
Ejusdem tractatus de subjectione & exemp. clericorum 1612
Ejusdem tractatus de jure connubiorum *Fran.* 1613
Azonis summa aurea juris civilis, 2 *Vol.* *Basil* 1596
Ejusdem comment. in codicem Justiniani 1595
Baronis tractatus de beneficiis *Colon* 1563
Balduinus de legibus ecclesiast. & civilibus constant.
Aurelii tractatus de rebus judicatis *Par.* 1611
Bronchurst miscellanea controversiarum *Lugd.*
Anton. Barbosa de canonicis & dignititabus *ibid.* 1664
Fran. Broei chronologia historica totius juris *Par.* 1622
Brummeri commentaria ad legem conciam 1668
Barbosæ tractatus de officio & potestate parœchi *Ven.* 1634
Bozzius de temporali ecclesiæ jurisdictione *Rom.* 1601
Bugnion tractatus de legibus abrogatis in Galliâ
Bonacossæ tractatus de famulis & servis *Ven.* 1575
De Bello Æconomia canonica *Lugd.* 1589

Bachovii tractatus de actionibus juris *Franc.* 1657
Ejusdem tractatus de pignoribus & hypothecis *ibid.* 1657
Beckmanni notitia dignitatum civilium *Franc.* 1685
Bertichii conclusiones practicabiles, 4 *Vol.*
Bertrandi tractatus de juris peritis *Tolos.* 1617
Barth. Baraterii reformatio feudorum per Rigattium edit. *Paris* 1641
Joh. Henr. Bergheri œconomia juris civilis *Lips.* 1712
Breweri tractatus de jure connubiorum 1665
Georg. Beyri delineationes juris civilis *Lips.* 1713
Jacobi à Carolo bibliotheca pontificia
Canisii summa juris canonici *Ingols.* 1600
Calvoli conclusiones in processibus judiciariis *Lips.* 1616
Carerii practica causarum criminalium *Franc.* 1600
Cantelii historia urbium metropoliticarum 1684
Conringius de origine juris Germanici *Helms.* 1649
Andreæ Crusii tractatus de jure offerendi 1661
Caroccii tractatus de juramento decisorio *Osnab.* 1676
Cajetan de comparation. de authoritate pap. & concilii
Chokier de jurisdictione ordinarii in exemptos. *Colon.* 1620
Cuvernon Archi-presbyter & decanus ruralis *Paris* 1646
Cujacii opera omnia juridica 5 *Vol.* *Franc.* 1596
Choppinus de privilegiis rusticorum *Paris* 1575
Coppen observationes juris practicæ *Franc.* 1678
Coleri tractatus de alimentis *Lips.* 1597
Capellæ tractatus de servitutibus

Mat.

Mat. Colerus de orig. progress. & utilit. juris Saxonici 1579

Costalii adversaria juris *Colon.* 1597

Christianæi leges civium Mechliensium *Antw.* 1625

Costani quæstiones juris memorabiles *Lugd.* 1558

Consuetudines Bituricenses *Paris* 1543

Anton. Contii opera omnia juridica *Ibid.* 1616

Craigii jus feudale tribus libris comprehensum *Lips.* 1716

Corvini juris-prudentiæ summarium ap. Elz. 1655

Codex juris feudalis Alemannici per Schilterum *Argent.* 1697

Cammanni Brunopolitani collegium polito-juridic. *Giessæ.* 1612

Collegium Lauterbachianum juris *Tubing.* 1713

Capellæ consilia criminalia *Lugd.* 1541

Marantæ consilia sive responsa juris 1599

Navarri consilia sive responsa juris 2 *Vol. Romæ.* 1602

Wamesii consilia sive responsa juris *Lovan.* 1606

Boerii decisiones juridicæ *Ven.* 1563

Genuæ decisiones de mercutura 1592

Manticæ decisiones rotæ Romanæ 1620

Riccii collectanea decisionum forensium 3 *Vol. Genev.* 1629

Seradori consilia sive responsa juris *Rom.* 1617

Decreta concilii Tridentini per Marzill. edita 1618

Decreta ordinum *Holland* & *Westfrisiæ* pro pace ecclesf. 1614

Didacus de Mendrandi de consensu connubiali 1650

Escobar de rationib. administratorum tractatus 1618

Epistolæ summ. pontificum per Gretserum editæ 1613

Epistola Francisci de Ingenuis de jurisd. Venetarum ad mare Adriat.

Eberlinus de origine juris & omnium magistratuum *Witteb.* 1672

Eugubinus de falsa donatione Constantini magni *Lugd.* 1547

Lybenii dissertatio de orig. & usu juris canonici *Helmst.* 1672

Petri de Ferrariis aurea praxis juris *Genev.* 1626

Fabri tractatus de alimentis 1628

Ejusdem comment. de diversis regulis juris 1618

Fuschus de visitatione ecclesiarum *Romæ* 1616

Forneri tractatus de verborum significatione. *Aurel.* 1584

Freheri Parerga sive observationes juris 1622

Francisci Florentis opera juridica *Paris* 1679

Freheri commentar. originum Palatinarum 1599

Fabri agonisticon sive de ludis veterum 1592

Anton. Faber de erroribus pragmatic. 4 *Vol.* 1595

Fachinæi controversiæ juris *Colon. Agr.* 1619

Ferrelii consilia & tractatus juris 1562

Johan. Felde de jure personarum & potestate. domestica. *Helmst.*

Pauli Fuschi singularia de jure Cæsar. & pontificio 1600

Flori tractatus de prohibitione duelli 1600

Forcatulus de occulta juris-prudentia 1549

Albericus Gentilis de verborum significatione *Han.* 1614, 1674

Ejusdem tractatus de legationibus *Lond.* 1585

Gulielmus Grotius de vitis jurisconsultorum *Lugd. Bat.* 1690

Scipio Gentilis ad legem Clodiam de vi comment. *Altd.* 1662

Goldastus de Bohemiæ ejusque provinciarum juribus 1627

An-

Andrææ Gail practicæ observationes juris *Col. Agr.* 1698

Garsias de expensis & meliorationibus *Lugd.* 1614

Gambacurta de immunitate ecclesiarum *Ibid.* 1622

Germonii tractatus de legatis principum, *&c.* *Rom.* 1627

Graswinkelii libertas Veneta *L. Bat.* 1634

Ejusdem tractatus de jure majestatis *Hag.* 1642

Groenwegen tractatus de legib. abrogat. in *Holland.* *Noviom.* 1677

Ejusdem tractatus de legib. abrogatis in *Hollandia* 1664

Guntherius de veteri jure pontificio urbis *Romæ,* *Paris* 1612

Gryphiander de insulis, & de mari, fluminibus, *&c.* 1607

Ejusdem tractatus de insulis, & de mari, fluminibus, *&c.* *Franc.* 1625

Gryphii volumen legum & statutorum, *Ven.* 1606

Gyphanii antimononiæ juris *Franc.*

Ejusdem tractatus de renuntiationibus *Ibid.* 1608

Gymnici practicæ observationes juris 1607

Jacobi Gothofredi fragmenta legum 12 Tab. legis Juliæ, *&c.* *Gen.* 1617

Haraldi Huitfeldi præfatio ad leges Scanicas 1590

Anton. Heringii de fidejussoribus tractatus 1647

Ulrici Huberi prælectiones ad jus Roman. cura Moncken. *Lips.* 1707

Casp. Henrici Hornii juris prudentia feudalis *Wittenb.* 1705

Haberti tractatus de primatu Petri *Paris* 1645

Joach. Hagemeir de authoritate jur. civil. & canonici 1663

Hottingeri tractatus de legibus Hæbræorum *Tigur* 1655

Hus-

Husson tractatus de advocato forensi *Paris* 1666
Hontemii tractatus de arte notariatus *Mog.* 1607
Justiniani novellæ per Julium Patricium *Brug.* 1565
Ernestus Kestnerus de defectibus juris comm. in German. 1708
Daniel. Keyseri historia juris civil. feud. & canonici 1693
Jacob. Labitte index legum omnium in pandectis *Par.* 1557
Thom. Lindemanni historia juris Romani *Rostoch.* 1627
Martin. Libergii universi juris historica descriptio *Pict.* 1567
Limnæi capitationes imperator. & regum Romano German. 1651
Lupi tractatus de libertate ecclesiastica, *&c.* *Argent.* 1561
Leonis Pontif. 3 Epistolæ ad Carolum magnum *Helmst.*
Joh. Petri Lydewig. dissertatio, jura feudis vicina complectens 1708
Matthæi tractatus de Nobilitate *L. Bat.* 1686
Ejusdem tractatus de jure gladii *ibid.* 1689
Mosaicarum & Romanarum legum collatio per Pithæum
Fredericus de Mendrano de Interdictis 1616
Marculphi formulæ veteres & lib. legum Salicarum 1665
Meyrer tractatus de Pignoribus & Hypothecis 1611
Marcellus de jure singulari Roman. pontificum 1627
Morini Exercitationes ecclesiasticæ de orig. Primat. *Par.* 1636

Marantæ praxis ſive de Ordine judiciario *Col. Ag.* 1650

Mynſinger Obſervationes ſingulares juris *Aur. Allob.* 1629

Ejuſdem comment. in Juſtiniani Inſtitutiones *Gen.* 1633

Magalianus de eccleſiaſtico principatu *Lugd.* 1609

Eric. Mauritii Diſſertatio de princip. juris publici *Tibeng.* 1655

Gerhard Van Maſtricht de Neglectu juris canon. ſtud. *Hal.* 1705

Juſti Meyeri collegium Argentorat. per Geor. Biccium *Argent.* 1667

Ejuſdem collegium Argentoratenſe, 3 *Vol. ibid.* 1657

Mandeſii praxis & Theoria commiſſionum *Ven.* 1585

Palæotus de Sacri Conſiſtorii conſultationibus *Ven.* 1594

Onuph. Panvinius de primatu Petri & ſedis Apoſtolicæ 1591

Polus (Cardinal.) de concilio generali *Romæ* 1562

Photii nomocanon cum comment. Balſamonis Græce *Paris* 1605

Beat. Parentis Syntagma juris feudalis *Franc.* 1717

Platus de Dignitate & officio Cardinalis *Rom.* 1602

Piccolus de Antiquo jure Eccleſiæ Siculæ *Meſſin.* 1623

Poncius de Impedimentis Matrimonii *Salman.* 1613

Anton. Peregrinus de Fidei-commiſſis *Lugd.* 1607

Philip. Paſchalis de viribus patriæ poteſtatis 1619

Franc. de Pavinis Baculus Paſtoralis ſeu de viſitationibus

Puf-

Puffendorf de jure Naturæ & Gentium tractat. *Amst.* 1704

Pancirollus de claris legum interpretibus *Ven.* 1655

Perezii comment. seu Scholia in Digesta *Amst.* 1669

Ejusdem Prælectiones in codicem Justinianæum *ibid.* 1671

Reusner de jure Testamentor & ult. voluntatum *Jenæ.* 1597

Ricterus de jure Successionis ab Intestato 1647

Conrad. Rittershusii in leges 12 tab. comment. *Argent.* 1616

Ejusdem differentiæ juris Civilis & Canonici 1638

Roussel Historia Jurisdictionis Pontificiæ *Par.* 1625

Ruffini legum Mosaicarum seu Judaicar. collectio *Gen.* 1593

Rebuffi tractatus de Privilegiis scholarium *Antw.* 1583

Joh. Robhahn. Palalipomena seu quæstiones juris, *&c.* *Arg.* 1672

Regino de Disciplinâ ecclesiasticâ veterum 1659

Reformatio legum Ecclesiasticar. ecclesiæ Anglican. *Lond.* 1640

Sam. Rachelii otium Noviomagense *Amst.* 1685

Sanctarellus de Hæresi, Schismat. & Apostasiâ, *&c.* 1625

Seldeni tractatus de Nuptiis & Divortiis *Lond.* 1646

Ejusdem tractatus de Synedriis, 3 *Vol.* *ibid.* 1679

Idem de Successionibus in bona ab intestato defuncti *ibid.* 1631

Ejusdem tractatus de jure Naturali & Gentium *Lips.* 1695

Ejuſdem tractatus de jure Naturali & Gentium *Argent.* 1663

Sbrozzii tractatus de officio & poteſtat. Vicarii gener. *Rom.* 1630

Simoncellus de Decretis in contractibus 1674

Scacciæ tractatus de Appellationibus 1663

Skneidwini comment. in Inſtitution. Juſtinian. *Arg.* 1632

Sam. Strykii uſus modernus pandectarum *Fran.* 1690

Ejuſdem continuatio uſus moderni pandectarum *Hal.* 1704

Ejuſdem continuatio à libro 22 uſq; *ibid.* 1710

Ejuſdem continuatio tertia uſus moderni pandect. *ibid.* 1713

Ejuſdem continuatio quarta ad finem uſq; pandect. *ibid.* 1713

Strauchius de Origin. libris & Authorit. juris canon. *Jenæ.* 1673

Sigonius de Antiquo jure Provinciarum *Vien.* 1568

Matthæi Stephani tractatus de jure Publico *Roſtoch.* 1624

Stockmanni tractatus de jure Devolutionis 1667

Seradori comment. ad primum & ſecundum librum Inſtitut. *Lipſ.* 1606

Summa Conſtitutionum ſumm. pontificum per Matth. *Lugd.* 1589

Summa Bullarii per Stephanum Quaranta *ibid.* 1622

Summa Cherubini Bullarii per Steph. Quaranta *Ven.* 1607

Synodus Florentina Græcè & Latinè *Floren.*

Sixtini tractatus de Regalibus *Caſell* 1617

Silvæ tractatus de Beneficiis *Paris* 1573

Sylvii comment. ad jus Romanum *ibid.* 1603

Sudorii Diſputationes civiles *ibid.* 1585

Spini à Caceres ſpeculum Teſtamentorum *Franc.* 1600
Sauterii tractatus de Fallitis *Leyd.* 1619
Sigonius de lege curiatâ ac jure Magiſtratum *Ven.* 1569
Schickardi jus regium Hebræorum *Argent.* 1625
Statuta Urbis Romanæ *Rom.* 1590
Siccamæ leges antiquæ Friſiorum *Franc.* 1617
Sarpi tractatus de jure Aſylorum *Leyd.* 1622
Seldeni Mare clauſum ſive de dominio Maris *ibid.* 1636
Thomaſius de Ratione habendi concilia *Rom.* 1565
Thomaſii Nævorum juris-prud. Rom. ante Juſtin. libri
Tholoſani tractatus de Republicâ *Fran.* 1600
Theureni tractatus de crimine luſæ Majeſtatis
Thomaſii Cautelæ de Præcognitis juris-prud. Ecclеſ. *Halæ.* 1712
Trivorii Obſervationes criticæ juris
Thomaſii Diſſertatio de originibus feudalibus *Hal.* 1710
Joh. de Turrecremata ſummæ de Eccleſiâ *Ven.* 1561
Theophili Inſtitutiones Græc. & Lat. per Fabrett. & Curt. *Par.* 1638
Rud. Volemari illuſtres quæſtiones juris 1613
Volumen Statutorum legum ac jurium Venetorum *Ven.* 1651
Vinnii Proceſſus judiciarius *Brem.* 1658
Ejuſdem comment. in Juſtiniani Inſtitution. *Amſt.* 1703
Du Vallius de poteſtate Papæ in eccleſiam 1614
Joh. Mart. Voight tractatus de Cambiis 1670
Vizzani tractatus de Mandatis principum 1656
Vitelii tractatus de contractibus Mulierum 1656

Usillus de Authoritate curiarum Præsidialium *Lugd.* 1556

Ugolini tractatus de Hæreticis *Romæ* 1568

Idem de censuris Romano Pontifici reservatis *Ven.* 1602

Wamesii tractatus de Appellationibus *Lovan.* 1606

Wisembecii comment. in pandectas juris *Amst.* 1665

Wolgang Tretmonii index legum omnium in pandect. content. *Par.* 1557

Ejusdem index seu Elenchus omnium Authorum sive Scriptorum tam in jure civili quam canonico comment. *Franc.* 1585

Zazii tractatus de Actionibus forensibus

Ziegleri tractatus de jure Majestatis *Witten.* 1681

Rein Zurich jus Maritimum Hanseaticum 1667

Ivonis Carnotensis Panormia

Zecchii tractatus de Beneficiis & Pensionibus *Veron.* 1601

Zyppæi notitia juris Belgici *Antw.* 1635

Burgundi consuetudines Flandriæ *L. Bat.* 1634

Berengarii tractatus de contrahendâ emptione *Lugd.* 1548

Budelii Authores varii de monetis *Colon* 1591

Balduinus de famosis libellis & de calumniatorib. *Paris* 1562

Brissonius de Ritu Nuptiarum & jure Connubiorum *ibid.* 1564

Bonacossæ Quæstiones criminales *Ven.* 1573

Bartoli Distinctiones juris *Basil* 1566

Jac. Bonjour Axiomata pandectarum *Lugd.* 1550

Borchotten comment. in Institutiones Justin. *Witten.* 1611

Balduini comment. in Institution. Justinian. *Paris* 1545

Brunellus in decretal. de homicidio & Election. Papæ 1518
Bullæ orationes & varia concilium Lateran. ſpectantia
Bullæi horæ ſubſecivæ *Brem.* 1621
Bertachini tractatus de Gabellis *Lugd.* 1533
Block tractatus de jure vectigalium *Baſil* 1617
Le Bret ordo perantiquus jurium Civilium *Paris* 1604
Brantius de Officio perfecti Senatoris *Antw.* 1633
Brederotii Lexicon juris
Blackvodæus contra Buchanan. de jure Regn. ap Scotos *Pict.* 1585
Coraſius de jure civili in Artem redigendo *Lugd.* 1560
Calvini Paratitla codicis è diverſ. Authorib. collecta *Fran.* 1612
Coſtani tractatus de dotibus & earum jure *Lugd.* 1556
Clementis Romani Conſtitutiones Apoſt. Græc. edit. per Turrian. 1563
Canones Apoſtolici cum Zonaræ comment. Gl. *Paris* 1558
Conſtitutiones Synodi Placentinæ ſub Cardin. de Aretio *Plac.* 1570
Concilia & Synodalia Decreta eccleſ. Rothom. per Pomeray *Roth.* 1577
Conſtitutiones Synodales diocæſ. Belvacenſis *Par.* 1531
Conſtitutiones Synodi Carnotenſis Sub D. de Thou. 1575
Concilium Duziacenſe editum à Collotio *Paris* 1658
Geſta conciliorum Moguntiaci & Wormiacenſ. *Baſil* 1532
Concilium provinciale Cameracenſe *Mont.* 1587

Canones Pænitentiales cum notis Auguſtini *Ven.* 1584

Antonii Contii Opera juridica, edit. per Merillium *Par.* 1616

D. Aveſan tractatus de contractibus, 2 *Vol.* *Aurel.* 1644, 1659

Damhouderii praxis Rerum civilium *Antw.* 1601

Decreta Provincialis Synodi Ravennat. ſub Cardinal Feltrio *Rom.* 1569

Decreta Synodi primæ Ariminenſis, A. D. 1577 *Bonon.* 1577

Dudiskii Oratio in concilio Trident. pro conjugio liber. *Offemb.* 1610

Decreta Synodalia eccleſiæ Pariſienſis *Paris* 1515

Damhouderii praxis rerum Criminalium *Antw.* 1617

Zeger Bern Van Eſpen tractatus Hiſtorico Canonic. *Leod.* 1693

Evengelius de Privilegiis juris civilis

Albericus Gentilis de donationib. inter virum & uxorem *Han.* 1604

Ejuſdem Diſputationes juridicæ *Lond.* 1603

Gothofredi tractatus de Salario *Genev.* 1666

Harmenopuli Epitome juris civilis Græcè *Paris* 1540

Ejuſdem Epitome juris civilis, Gl. cum Gothofred. Not. *Genev.* 1587

Ulrici Hunnii Reſolutiones juris civilis *Franc.* 1620

Jordanus de Majorib. epiſcopor. cauſis ad Papam deferend. *Ven.* 1572

Gerbais de Majoribus epiſcoporum cauſis *Paris* 1679

Hartmanni Quæſtiones juris Roman. & Saxonic. 5 *Vol.* *Heid.* 1604

Imberti Institutiones Forenses Galliæ *Paris* 1545
Labbæi omnium conciliorum Synopsis historica *ibid.* 1661
Simon à Lewen censura forensis 1678
Lupi tractatus de Appellationibus *Brux.* 1683
Loccenius de jure Maritimo & Navali *Helmſ.* 1651
Leonis Thesaurus Fori ecclesiastici *Rom.* 1616
Limnæus de jure Publico Romano-Germanico, 5 *Vol.* 1657
Christian Liebenthal jus Fœderis Giessæ 1624
Merulæ Synopsis praxeos juris civilis *Graven.* 1631
Meyeri Collegium juridicum 1617
Meursii tractatus de legibus Atticis *Traject.* 1683
Mossi tractatus de Contractibus *Colon* 1614
Mundii tractatus de Comitibus Palatinis
Molleri comment. ad Consuetudines Saxonicas *Lipſ.* 1610
Messenii leges Gothorum & Suecorum *Stockh.* 1614
Muscatelli praxis civilis regni Neapolitani *Ven.* 1600
Molinæus de Donationibus in contract. Matrimon. *&c.* *Lugd.* 1551
Molinæus de Commerciis, contractibus & Usuris *Paris* 1608
Menilii Paratitla juris civilis Universi *Carolop.* 1651
Mandosi Formularium curiæ Romanæ *Romæ* 1574
Petrus de Marca de Concordiâ Sacerdotii & Imperii *Paris* 1641
Mathurini Montani comment. in Novellas *Lugd.* 1549
Garciæ Mastrilli Decisiones juris, 3 *Vol.* 1660
Paschalii tractatus de Legato *Paris* 1612
Pithæi Opera juridica & historica 1666
Privilegia academiæ Lovaniensis *Leodii.* 1665
Cyprian Regneri ab Oosterga censura Belgica *Traject.* 1669

Ro-

Raguelli leges Politicæ ex Scriptur. ſacr. collectæ *Par.* 1615

Raguelli comment. ad Deciſiones Juſtiniani *ibid.* 1610

Marcelli vulpe praxis judicialis Fori eccl.

OCTAVO.

Corpus juris civilis, 15 *Vol.* *Lugd.* *Rovil.* 1571

Corpus juris civil. ad Exemplar. Haloandri, 6 *Vol.* *Par.*

Corpus juris civilis, 9 *Vol.* 12 *Tom.* *Paris* 1560

Corpus juris civilis, 2 *Vol.* ap. Elziv. *Amſt.* 1664

Corpus juris civilis, 9 *Vol.* *Gen.* *Vign.* 1580

Corpus juris civilis, cum Not. Ruſſardi, 4 *Vol.* *Plantin.* 1568

Alciati Aurea praxis utriuſque juris *Col.* 1555

Ejuſdem tractatus de Præſumptionibus *Lugd.* 1538

Ærodii tractatus de Patrio jure *Ultraj.* 1671

Ejuſdem libellus Decretorum *Paris* 1573

Antonius Auguſtinus de legib. & Senatus-conſultis *Rom.* 1583

Apelli Tyrocinia juris diſtinctionib. repetit. *Baſil*

Bernard. Autumni cenſura Gallica in jus civile Rom. *Par.* 1616

Annæi Rob. Aurelii rerum Judicatarum tractatus *Lugd.* 1620

Roland. D'Avalle tractat. de Confection. Inventarii 1632

D'Aveſan tractatus de Sponſalib. & divortiis *L. Bat.* 1670

Bronchurſtii Enantiaphanôn centuria *Hard.* 1652

Eni-

Enimund. Bonefidii libri tres jur. Oriental ap. H. Steph. 1573
Borcholten commentar. de Rebus creditis *Helmſ.* 1596
Ejuſdem commentar. de Tranſactionibus *ibid.* 1593
Ejuſdem comment. de acquirend. & omittend. Poſſeſſion. *ibid.* 1592
Ejuſdem commentar. de jure-jurando *ibid.* 1593
Ejuſdem commentar. de in litem jurando *ibid.* 1593
Ejuſdem commentar. de Nautico Fœnore *ibid.* 1594
Ludov. Benderi tractat. de Reviſione actuum *Franc.* 1589
Hen. Brinkmanni Pandectæ juris civilis *Amſt.* 1708
Bronchurſtii methodus Feudorum *Ultraj.* 1652
Baumani tractatus de Sequeſtris 1597
Barbari Veneti tractatus de re Uxorâ
Bertrandi tractatus de juris-peritis antiquis *L. Bat.* 1675
Ejuſdem tractatus de Nuptiis ſecundis
Beſoldi tractatus de Appellationibus
Babbi tractatus de Præſcriptionibus
Bertrandi Βίοι νομικῶν ſeu de jurisper. Antiquis *L. Bat.* 1575
Bezæ tractatus de Polygamiâ & divortiis 1568
Beloji tractatus de jure civili Romanor. *Paris* 1583
Bindfeldii tractatus de Injuriâ & damno dato 1595
Briſſonii juris civilis Antiquitates *Heid.* 1664
Bruſſii principia juris Feudalis *Edinb.* 1713
Budæi tractatus de Aſſe *Colon* 1528
Burchardus de Hodiernæ juris-prudentiæ Nævis *Han.* 1682

Caballini tractatus de Commerciis & Usuris *Ven.* 1576

Jon. de Canibus tractatus de Executoribus 1590

Carbonis Practica practicarum *Franc.* 1599

Carerius de Deposito, Oblationibus & Sequestro 1594

Casoni tractatus de Maleficiis 1584

Canisii tractatus de Sponsalibus *Ingolst.* 1622

Christenius de causis Matrimonialibus *Arnh.* 1663

Philip. de Casalis de Testament. & ultim. voluntat. *Agri.* 1598

Casæ tractatus de modo Articulandi & Probandi 1598

Cotoræus de jure & privilegiis militum *Aug. Trev.* 1610

Chapeuaville tractatus de Casibus reservatis

Corasius de Officiis, dignitatib. & beneficiis Eccles. 1596

Corrasius & Hopperus de Arte juris 1582

Corvini juris Feudalis tractatus *Lugd.* 1654

Ejusdem Enchiridion seu Institut. Imperial. *Amst.* 1640

Ejusdem tractatus de jure Canonico *ibid.* 1657

Corvini Digesta per Aphorismos *ibid.* 1656

Campianus de Divortio Henrici octavi Angliæ *Antw.* 1631

Constantini comment. de Legib. ecclesiast. & civil. *Arg.* 1612

Jacob. Cujacii collectio juris Feudalis *Colon.* 1588

Cujacii Paratitla in libros Digestorum *ibid.* 1577

Covarruvias de jure Pontificio & Cæsareo 1565

Caroli Magni & Ludovici Pii Leges ecclesiasticæ 1640

Julius Clarus de jure Emphyteutico *Colon* 1575

Caii Institutiones & Pauli sentent. per Bouchard. *Lov.* 1573

Co-

Cowellii Institutiones juris Anglicani *Oxon.* 1675
Dalvin. tractatus de potestate Episcoporum
Duareni tractatus de ecclesiæ Ministeriis 1559
Ejusdem tractatus de beneficiis Ecclesiastic. *Lugd.* 1585
Donzellini remedium ferendarum Injuriarum *L. Bat.* 1635
Johan. Doviatii Historia juris canonici *Paris* 1676
Duck de usu & authoritate jur. Roman. civil. *Lond.* 1679
Justi Eccardi explicatio Legis regiæ
Everardi loci argumentorum legalium 1648
Epitome processus in occidendis Hæreticis
Ficheri tractatus de Famâ publicâ *Basil* 1591
Flaminei de Rubeis tractatus de Adulteriis 1645
Fenestellæ tractatus de Magistratibus *Romæ* 1591
Floridus Sabinus de jur. civil. interpretibus
Figuli Lexion juris civilis 1549
Forsteri Historia juris civilis *Helms.* 1609
Freighus de Logica juris consultorum
Ferrarii Annotation. ad juris utriusq; titulos 1544
Fran. Florens de rectâ jur. canonici discendi ratione 1632
Meynardi disputationes de juribus episcoporum *Aug. Pict.* 1612
Gothofredus de ratione ordinis in pandect. cod. *&c.* 1580
Vincent Gravina de ortu & progressu juris civilis *Lips.* 1708
Grævii Enchiridion de principiis jur. natural.
Gothofredi Manuale juris *L. Bat.* 1676
Alberic. Gentilis de libris juris civilis & canonici
Ejusdem Disputationes de Nuptiis *Han.* 1601
Ejusdem tractatus de Legationibus
Scipio Gentilis de bonis Maternis & secundis Nuptiis *Han.* 1606

Ejus-

Ejuſdem tractatus de Juriſdictione *ibid.* 1601
Ejuſdem tractatus de Conſpirationibus *Han.* 1602
Ejuſdem tractatus de Alimentis 1600
Ejuſdem parerg. ad pandectas *Franc.* 1588
Gilhauſen comment. de Injuriis & Famoſ. libellis *Lich.* 1602
Alberic. Gentilis de armis Romanorum *Han.* 1612
Ejuſdem tractatus de jure belli *ibid.* 1558
Goddæi comment. de contrahend. & committ. ſtipulat. 1612
Garciæ tractatus de ultim. fine jur. civ. & canon. *Colon* 1585
Gigantis tractatus de Penſionibus eccleſiaſticis *Colon, A.* 1619
Lud. Gomez in regulas Cancellariæ 1547
Gabrielis Concluſiones communes juris 1600
Grotius de jure Belli & Pacis, notis Gronov. *Amſt.* 1702
Glanvil tractatus de Legibus Angliæ 1673
Nicol. Hennelius de veteribus juris conſultis *Lipſ.* 1654
Hemmingii tractatus de Lege naturæ *Wittemb.* 1577
Heraldi tractatus de rerum judicatarum authoritate
Hopperi Paratitlum juris civilis Romanorum *Colon* 1580
Juſtiniani Inſtitutiones ab Accurſio *Lugd.* 1570
Ejuſdem Inſtitutiones, apud Elzivir 1654
Inſtrucca politica de Legados *Amb.* 1656
Kirkneri tractatus de Legato *Lichæ.* 1604
Loccenii Sueciæ regni Leges provinciales 1675
Luccenius de jure Maritimo & Navali *Helmſ.* 1650
Simon Van Lewen de origin. & progreſſ. jur. Roman. *L. B.* 1672

Lutii

Lutii tractatus de Privilegiis ſtudentium *Franc.* 1625

Manutii Antiquitat. Romanæ & de Legibus, ap. Aldum 1557

Ejuſdem Antiquitates Romanæ & Legibus 1582

Meynardi Diſputationes de juribus epiſcoporum *Aug. Pict.* 1612

Petrus de Marca de veterib. Canonum collectionib. *Paris* 1681

Maſuerii tractatus de practicâ Forenſi *Lugd.* 1597

Mandoſius de Monitoriis & Inhibitionibus *Spiræ.* 1587

Molinæi tractatus de Donationibus *Lugd.* 1556

Seb. de Medicis tractatus de Legibus, ſtatut. *&c.* 1574

Fabiani de Monte tractat. de empt. & venditione *Ven.* 1584

Peckii tractatus de Eccleſiis reparandis

Joh. Pacii Legum conciliatorium *Lugd.* 1643

Fran. Polleti hiſtoria Fori Romani, per Broidæum 1579

Ejuſdem hiſtoria Fori Romani, per eundum 1587

Platæi regulæ generales juris *Lugd.* 1589

Practica Criminalis per Ignat. Lopez

Pratique & Maniere de proceder. en cauſ. crim. & civ. 1573

Porcellini tractatus de Inventario *Col. Agr.* 1590

Franc. de Ripa de Privilegiis contractuum *ibid.* 1590

Rodolphini tractatus de Arte notarii 1565

Stephani tractatus de Nobilitate civili 1590

Socini regulæ & Fallentiæ juris *Colon* 1626

Salmaſii ad jus Atticum & Roman. obſervat. *Leyd.* 1645

Ejuſdem tractatus de modo Uſurarum, *&c. ibid.* 1639

Tho-

Tholosani tractatus de Republicâ
Vantius de nullitatibus Processuum & sententiar. *Ven.* 1585
Wesembecii utriusq; juris Oeconomia *Par.* 1573
Zouchæi Quæstiones juris *Lond.* 1682
Ejusdem Elementa juris
Idem de jure inter gentes
Losæi tractatus de jure Universitatum 1627
Puffendorf elementa juris-prudentiæ 1672
Koleri Methodus de jure Emphyteutico *Ursin.* 1599
Blanci tractatus de Compromissis *Franc.* 1597
Ejusdem practica Criminalis *ibid.* 1577
Filesaca de Parœciarum & Parœcorum origine *Par.* 1608
Ejusdem tractat. de sacrâ episcoporum authoritate *ibid.* 1606
Imberti Enchiridion juris scripti Galliæ *Lugd.* 1556
Stephanus de Jurisdictione Judæor. Græcor. Romanor, *&c.* *Fran.* 1604
Seldenus de Successionibus ad leges Hæbræorum Elziver 1638
Pratei juris-prudentia vetus seu Dracon. & Solon. leg. *Lugd.* 1559
Capitula seu decreta Childebert. & Clothar. lex Salica, *&c.* *Paris* 1573
Statuta Veneta cum practica judiciali *Venet.* 1528
Buchananus de jure regni apud Scotos 1579
Theod. Zawakei speculum Senator. & official. regn. Polon. 1616
Tancredi tractat. de ordine judiciario *Colon* 1564
Hotoman. tripartita de leg. 12 tabular. comment. *Lugd.* 1564
Theodori Marcilii collect. & interpret. legum 12 tabul. *Paris* 1600

Cujacii

Struvii jus canonicum 1688
Cujacii Observationes juris *Col. Ag.* 1598
Ejusdem paratitla in libros Digestorum *Col.* 1577
Car. Labbæi Observation. & Emendat. in Synopsim Basil. *Par.* 1606
Randulph. Pratei juris-prudentia Media *Lugd.* 1561
Caii Institutiones juris per Viselium *L. Bat.* 1658
Gutherus de Officiis domûs Aug. pub. & privatæ *Lips.* 1672
Carpzovii Decisiones Saxoniæ ducum *Jenæ.* 1669

LIBRI OMISSI.

HUNNII variar. Resolutionum juris Civ. libri 4 *Franc.* 1620
Franc. Broæi Expositiones ad 4 libros Institut. *Par.* 1622
Ejusdem Chronologica historia totius juris *Par.*
Nicol. Eymerici directorium Inquisitorum *Ven.* 1607
Hen. de Bovick tractatus de jure Patronatus *Franc.* 1581
Ejusdem Distinctiones super 5 libros Decretal *Lugd.* 1498
Merc. Mant. Benevid. tractat. de jure Proligmisces *Franc.* 1588
Bertrandi consiliorum octo volumina *ibid.* 1603
Besoldi Conclusiones de jure universo *Tubin.* 1621
Idem de Comitibus & Baronibus imper. German. *ibid.* 1619

Filesaca de Paræciarum & Paræcorum orig. *Par.* 1608
Idem de Sacrâ Episcoporum authoritate *ibid.* 1606
Johan. Eichelius de varia Fortunâ juris civilis
Ludewig de jure Clientelari Germanorum
Eybenius de electis Feudalibus
Hornius de juris prudentia Feudali Longobardo-Teutonico 1705
Schilterus de Curiis dominicalibus
Anton. Dominicus de Prærogativâ allodiali, 4to. *Par.* 1645
Bohmeri tractatus de Feudis Ecclesiasticis
Marc. Antonius de Dominis de Republ. eccl.
Theodori Beltrii Dissertationes de Consistorio
Leyrenius de Vicariis episcoporum
Æneæ Sylvii comment. de Concilio Basil. *Col.* 1534
Simon Schardius de authoritate & juris prud. Imperiali 1609
Hertii tractatus de Feudis oblatis
Valerius Climentillus de Honore Bisellii
Schilteri Dissertatio de Naturâ & Origin. jur. publici
Sulpicii seu Kulpicii Dissertatio de studio juris recti instituendo, deq; scriptoribus eo pertinentibus 1700
Speculum juris Saxonici
Caspar Zieglerus de juribus Majestatis
Ericus Mauritius de principiis juris Germanici
Franc. Connani libri Com. juris civilis, 2 Tom. *Par.* 1553
Martin. Magorus à Schonberg de Advocatiâ Armatâ
Mastrillii tractatus de Magistratib. & eorum Imper. *Lugd.* 1621
Tiraquelli tractatus de Primogeniturâ

Strykii

Strykii Usus modernus juris Romani, in 4 Partes
Adrian Beyræi Syiloge Professorum Jenensium
Joh. Zeumerus de vitis Professorum juris
Joach. Hoppii Discursus præliminalis de Usu & Auth. juris civilis Romanorum
Itterus de Gradibus Academicis
Wintherus de Privilegiis doctorum
Harprecht Dissertatio de Mortuario
Kieffer tractatus de Judicaturâ Imperatoris
Antonius D'Atticus de Pace publicâ
Besoldi Thesauro-Practicus juridicus
Tarnovius de Feudis Megalopolitanis
Johan. de Filesacus de publicâ Pœnitentiâ Ecclesiasticâ
Johan. Frid. Knorrius de pub. Pœnitentiâ Ecclesiasticâ
Johan. Morini tractatus de Pœnitentiâ
Anton. Mincuccii Collectio Feudalis per Schilterum 1695
Johan. Frideric Rhœtius de juris publici Institutionib.
Lucius Assilius Regulus de Donationibus
Herman. Hormis Fasciculus juris publici
Caspar Ziegler de Origin. & Increment. juris Canonici
Frider. Schenck Interpretation. in 3 libros juris Feudalis 1555
Philippus Burchardus de hodiernæ juris-prudentiæ Nævis *Han.* 1682
Practica Criminalis Canonica per Ignat. Lopez 1593
Matthæi de Afflictis Decisionis Neapolitanæ *Lugd.* 1552
Schilteri Codex juris Feudalis Alemannici *Argent.* 1697

Boati

Beati Parentis Syntagma Feudale 1717

Fran. Hotomanni comment. de Feudis tripartita *Colon* 1573

Bulgarus & Placent. de Regulis juris *Col. Ag.* 1587

Fran. Balduini Justinianus sivè de jure nov. comment. *Bas.* 1560

Lexicon juridicum apud J. Stoer. 1594

Brissonii juris civilis Antiquitates *Heidel.* 1664

Osiandri Observationes in Grotium de jure Belli, 2 *Vol.* *Tub.* 1671

Nic. Vigelii Methodus juris Pontificii *Basil* 1616

Vigelii tractatus de causis Matrimonialibus *ibid.* 1575

Zepperi legum Mosaicarum explicatio

Albericus Gentilis de libris jur. civil. canon. *Han.* 1605

Gravina de Ortu & Progressu juris civil. 2 *Vol.* 1713

Hunoldi Plettenberg Introductio ad jus canon. *Heidel.* 1692

Philippi Burchardi Discursus de hodierna juris prudentiæ Nævis

Ejusdem Discursus de juris prudentia papizante *Pict.* 1711

Adam Riccius de librorum juris Roman. quantitate & qualitate 1635

Gulielmus Benedictus de Authoritate jur. civilis *Lugd.* 1654

Holfricus Ulric. Hunnius de Authoritate juris civ. *Giessæ.* 1629

F I N I S.